PHIL GORDON'S

LITTLE BLUE

BOOK

*More Lessons and Hand Analysis
in No Limit Texas Hold'em*

by Phil Gordon

SIMON SPOTLIGHT ENTERTAINMENT
New York   London   Toronto   Sydney

This publication contains the opinions and ideas of its author. It is intended to provide helpful and informative material on the subjects addressed in the publication. It is sold with the understanding that the authors and publisher are not engaged in rendering any kind of personal professional services in the book. The reader should consult a competent professional before adopting any of the suggestions in this book or drawing inferences from it.

The authors and publisher specifically disclaim all responsibility for any liability, loss or risk, personal or otherwise, which is incurred as a consequence, directly or indirectly, of the use and application of any of the contents of this book.

Certain individuals described in this book are fictionalized.

SSE

SIMON SPOTLIGHT ENTERTAINMENT
An imprint of Simon & Schuster
1230 Avenue of the Americas, New York, New York 10020
Copyright © 2006 by Phil Gordon
All rights reserved, including the right of reproduction in whole
or in part in any form.
SIMON SPOTLIGHT ENTERTAINMENT and related logo are
trademarks of Simon & Schuster, Inc.
Book design by Yaffa Jaskoll
Manufactured in the United States of America
First Edition 10 9 8 7 6 5 4 3 2 1
Library of Congress Cataloging-in-Publication Data
Gordon, Phil, 1970-
Phil Gordon's little blue book: more lessons and hand analysis in no limit
Texas hold'em / by Phil Gordon.   p. cm.
ISBN-13: 978-1-4169-2719-8   ISBN-10: 1-4169-2719-0
1. Poker. I. Title.   GV1251.G657 2006   795.412—dc22
2006015526

DEDICATION

To Barb

No matter how many times
my pocket aces get cracked,
with you in my life
I'll always be
the luckiest guy on the planet.

I love you very much.

CONTENTS

FOREWORD

PHIL GORDON:
PROFESSIONAL, AMBASSADOR,
TEACHER . . . AND FRIEND
BY CHRIS FERGUSON

I've heard Phil Gordon say things like, "I'm not the best player in the world." He has said it in conversations with me and with other pros, on the second page of the *Little Green Book*, and probably in this book as well. I'm not sure if that even counts as being humble, but Phil can afford to be humble.

He retired from business at twenty-eight, traveled the world, raised millions for philanthropic causes, authored two bestselling books, released a successful instructional DVD, hosted *Celebrity Poker Showdown*, and created a series of podcasts at the 2005 *World Series of Poker* that were among the most downloaded since that form of media began.

On top of all that, Phil is no slouch at the table. He finished fourth in the main event of the *World Series of Poker* in 2001 and has made four other World Series final tables, including two in 2005. It is unlikely he will go much longer without another chance to win his first bracelet—or several. He was also one of the first stars of the *World Poker Tour*, winning the pro division at the first *WPT* Aruba tournament and winning the *WPT* Bay 101 Shooting Stars championship.

Phil is less modest about his accomplishments as a teacher, but, again, his record speaks for itself. His instructional video and his two poker books, *Poker: The Real Deal* and *Phil Gordon's Little Green Book*, have taught hundreds of thousands of players to understand how professionals evaluate the game. As host of *Celebrity Poker Showdown*, he educated millions of viewers on how to analyze poker decisions.

Phil has also played an important role in transforming the image of poker. Go back ten years to when

I started playing in tournaments. Who would ever admit to being a professional? If someone said he played poker professionally, you felt sorry for him, or you were afraid of him.

Look how much that has changed. We are celebrities now. If I tell someone I'm a professional poker player, they might actually be impressed. Now they want to know how to become pros themselves.

Televised poker shows are responsible for this transformation. *Celebrity Poker Showdown*, which has shown millions of people that celebrities play poker, is responsible. Having all those viewers associate "professional poker player" with "Phil Gordon"—a smart, articulate gentleman who always communicates how to play a poker hand (or, as was more often the case on that show, how *not* to play a poker hand)—is responsible. A lot of other things are responsible too. But Phil was such a fixture on that show through 2005 that it's easy to take for granted how many people were introduced to poker through that show. Phil Gordon was many people's first image of a professional poker player . . . and he did a fantastic job of representing our game.

Phil and I have been talking about poker hands for a decade now, since long before we met face-to-face. During the midnineties, in the early days of the Internet, we communicated through rec.gambling.poker, which was then a small band of games-obsessed computer guys (and girls) who loved poker and wanted to get better at it.

So what was it like when we finally met at the 2001 *World Series of Poker* main event? Was it some kind of big occasion, with me, the reigning champion, finally shaking hands with this new star, who had just made the final table and was on the fast track to multimedia stardom?

No, it was nothing like that! We were still just two guys who loved poker and wanted to play better. I am flattered when Phil describes me as a "mentor." He is definitely one of the small number of professionals with whom I enjoy discussing poker hands and poker strategy. Together we have talked about a lot of hands and a lot of approaches to how to play them. Phil has told me that he has benefited a lot from those talks. I know I have.

I really enjoy those kinds of discussions. That is how we improve as players: analyzing our experiences, getting to hear about what other players are thinking and doing, testing our ideas, and refining and improving (and sometimes abandoning) those ideas.

Phil Gordon and I have a similar approach to the game of poker. I see Phil as an aggressive, solid player who is nevertheless not afraid to commit a lot of chips without the nuts. My play could also be described that way.

More important, though, we both believe that the way you improve at poker is not by finding answers. It is by finding *questions*. And one thing I know Phil can do is show you how to analyze a hand and ask yourself the right questions. That method will help you in every kind of situation and improve your chances of coming up with the right decision.

The best way to learn poker is to play it and talk about it with your friends. With this book think of Phil as your first friend in this process. Listen to how a professional thinks his way through a hand—not just the hands he played right but also the ones he played wrong. Do some thinking of your own. What would you do and, more important, *why*? Then do some talking and some listening: Find people you respect, and talk about poker hands and poker strategy. If you are a winning player, this can make you a bigger winning player. If you are a losing player, maybe it can turn you into a winner. If nothing else, talking about poker will be cheaper than losing at poker.

Phil and I have covered a lot of ground since that meeting in 2001. We have traveled the world together, celebrated each other's successes, commiserated about and analyzed each other's failures, watched poker's popularity skyrocket, tried to contribute to that phenomenon, and tried to benefit from it.

Our accomplishments in poker don't count for anything when we are at the table. Of course, it makes me happy if opponents are intimidated by me and let me steal when I have nothing, and give me action when I have the nuts, but that can't be the basis for any future success. All you really have at the poker table is your ability to make a good decision, and a willingness to learn and improve. So when I tell you that this book could be your key to entering "our world," I don't mean the VIP room at some hot nightclub or even some televised final table.

"Our world" is the world of ideas. To get in, you need a love of poker and a desire to improve. Phil Gordon has that desire. I have that desire. And, since you are reading this book, you obviously do too. You're well on your way.

And who knows? If you take Phil's advice to heart and combine it with experience, your own ideas, and a willingness to improve your thinking about poker strategy, maybe you will see us in those other places as well.

Welcome to our world!

ACKNOWLEDGMENTS

This book would not exist without my good friend and collaborator Jonathan Grotenstein. Our first literary effort, *Poker: The Real Deal*, was published in October 2004 amid the crazy, meteoric rise in popularity of the game. That work has since sold more than a hundred thousand copies and improved the game of many people across the world. Jonathan is the expert wordsmith who helps me convey my complex (and sometimes twisted) thoughts and ideas with clarity, consistency, and humor. A huge thank-you to Jonathan.

I'd also like to give kudos to the biggest group

of degenerate gamblers in the world, the Tiltboys: Rafe Furst, Dave "Diceboy" Lambert, Steve Miranda, Perry Friedman, Paul Swiencicki, Tony Glenning, Kim Scheinberg, John Kullmann, Josh Paley, Michael Stern, Lenny Augustine, Bruce Hayek, and Russ Garber. We've been playing poker together for fifteen years. Wednesday nights are nearly a religious experience for our group and by far the best night of the week. Our games of "Spit-and-Shit Ding-a-Ling-with-a-Twist" and high-stakes Roshambo (think $1,000 a throw . . . yes, we're sick) are legendary in our own minds. For an in-depth look at psychopathic degeneracy, check out the Tiltboy Web site, www.tiltboys.com, or pick up a copy of our book, *Tales from the Tiltboys*. Your life will never be the same.

My fiancée and future wife (redundantly redundant!), Barb Smith, deserves enormous amounts of credit for putting up with me, handling the massive swings in my mood (and bankroll), and being my biggest fan. She's also one hell of a good poker player. This book wouldn't exist without Barb's constant encouragement, support, and love. I've been lucky at the tables plenty of times—I've managed more than my fair share of 45–1 long-shot suckouts. But marrying Barb will be, by far, the biggest and luckiest suckout of my life.

Thanks to all of my family and my future in-laws,

as well as my godchildren (who love to see their names in print): Quinn and Savannah Averitt, Ben Philip Leader, Winnie and Charlie Swiencicki. I love you all.

At the poker table my job is to surround myself with the most mentally challenged people I can find and take their money. In business it is just the opposite: I do my best to surround myself with the smartest people I can find. My business manager, Alex Alvarez, inspires me to do everything better, and her time, energy, focus, and professionalism allow me to do so. My accountant, Marissa Chien, keeps me "in the money." My literary agents, Greg Dinkin and Frank Scatoni at Venture Literary, somehow convinced the smart people at Simon Spotlight Entertainment to take another shot with me, our third effort to date. Speaking of Simon Spotlight, thanks to all the folks there: Tricia Boczkowski, Jen Bergstrom, Jen Robinson, Nekiesha Walker, Russell Gordon, Yaffa Jaskoll, Rick Richter, Emily Westlake, and Frank Fochetta.

In every poker player's life there are people who bring him along, sharing their knowledge, secrets, and experiences. My friends at FullTiltPoker.com are without a doubt the best players in the world. Their tutelage and friendship is, in large part, responsible for my success in poker. Howard Lederer, Phil Ivey, John Juanda, Eric Seidel, Erick Lindgren, Jennifer Harman, and Andy

Bloch are always willing to talk about hands, rejoice in successes, and sympathize with bad beats. Many of these incredibly talented players have read through this book and suggested corrections and improvements. A very special thanks to my good friend Chris "Jesus" Ferguson, who took an extraordinary amount of time to coach me during the last five years. He also wrote one hell of a foreword to this book. If there is one player in the world I strive to emulate, it's Chris. Unfortunately, I look like crap in a cowboy hat, and growing my hair three feet long is not an option. Still, at the tables, Chris's game is the nuts.

Thanks to my business partners at my company, Expert Insight: Rafe Furst, Michael Keller, Bill Dougherty, and all of our other employees and partners. This work is in large part an extension of the Expert Insight mission: to allow the reader to "Get Inside the Mind of the Expert."™ If you haven't seen our innovative, experiential approach to teaching, I encourage you to pick up a copy of my instructional DVD *Final Table Poker* at www.expertinsight.com.

Thanks to Doug Donohue, who created my favorite poker simulator, DDPoker (www.ddpoker.com), Sebastiano DiBari and Sector Watches (www.sectorwatches. com), Bluff Magazine (www.bluffmagazine.com), Andrew Feldman and ESPN.com (www.espn.com/poker), and all my other poker-business partners.

My great-aunt Elizabeth "Lib" Lucas taught me to play poker when I was seven. She died of cancer the day I won my first major poker tournament. Every hand I play and tournament I enter, I dedicate to her. A portion of the proceeds from this book will be donated to the Cancer Research and Prevention Foundation (CRPF) in her memory. Poker players around the world are donating one percent of their tournament winnings to CRPF, and to date we've raised more than $1,000,000 through poker-related fund-raising efforts. Please, join us in putting a Bad Beat on Cancer: www.badbeatoncancer.org. Autographed copies of this book and my other works, and personal phone lessons are available in exchange for donations on this Web site.

Finally, and hopefully without seeming like a tremendous suck-up, I want to thank you, my readers. I thank you for your interest in the game that I've made a profession. I thank you for continuing to learn and stretch your game. I thank you for the investment you've made in me as a sort of mentor and teacher. I thank you for the kind words, reviews, e-mails, and autograph requests. I thank you for your donations to the Cancer Research and Prevention Foundation. I wish you all continued success, at and away from the tables.

INTRODUCTION

"Poker theory" is great, but poker is not about theory, diagrams, flowcharts, or checklists. Poker is all about what happens at the table: a good read, a tough lay-down, a mathematically correct call, a big bluff, a timely all-in. For me poker is about making difficult, winning decisions at the table. When you get home from poker night, your significant other doesn't ask, "Hey, did you learn any poker theory tonight?" He or she asks you if you *won*. If they're really great partners, they'll even ask, and listen to you talk, about specific hands—even bad-beat stories.

1

After the publication and overwhelming success of my *Little Green Book*, I have received thousands of e-mails from around the world. Nearly everyone who wrote to me managed to pick up some bit of poker theory from the book. Kudos to all who improved: You were able to successfully take theory and apply it in practice—that is a true achievement. I can't begin to tell you how great it feels to help people become better players—I truly enjoy teaching poker more than I enjoy playing poker.

If you're the kind of person who prefers the practical to the theoretical, however, then this book should help you enormously. Inside you'll find several dozen hands from actual play, fully annotated. The goal in each hand is to take you *inside my mind* and let you read my thoughts as the hands play out.

Some of the hands are taken from tournaments you may have seen me play on television. I've been very fortunate to win two *World Poker Tour* events; many of the key hands from those tournaments are replayed here for you. So are many hands from the various *World Series of Poker* events I've participated in, including the highly entertaining final table at the 2001 *WSOP* championship (where I was lucky enough to finish fourth).

Not all the hands presented here leave me beaming with pride. Yes, I'm nearly certain that I could have found thousands of hands that I've played exactly right: I've won plenty of massive pots, and I've made plenty of great reads and laydowns. But some of the hands that have been most important to my success as a player aren't the hands that I've won but the hands that I've lost by playing poorly or overlooking a better play. These instructive hands—and there are plenty in this book—taught me valuable lessons about the game of No Limit Texas Hold'em. I hope these hands will help your game as well.

While reading this book, you're not going to agree with all the plays that I made. Good! As most professionals will tell you, there are many different ways to play a winning game of No Limit Texas Hold'em. I am not the best Hold'em player in the world, but I am a winning player—I've been a professional since 1997 and I've never had a losing year. I've won (and lost) playing the hands exactly the way I've represented them here and in my *Little Green Book*, but that doesn't make me the authoritative voice. . . . If you disagree with the way I've played a hand, you may very well be right. There are many hands, in retrospect, that I might (and should) have played differently as well. The point is to think about why I'm right or wrong and, in doing so, expand your own ability to analyze a situation at the poker table.

As you're reading, keep this in mind: I do not consider myself a gambler. Nearly every day people e-mail me or stop me on the street and ask me: "What's it like to be a professional gambler?" I invariably answer the same way each time: "I've never gambled a day in my life." I consider myself a strategic investor. For every $100 I put into the pot, I expect to take more than $100 back out. If I can succeed more times than not, hand after hand, tournament after tournament, and year after year, I ensure a long-term positive expectation. That positive expectation applied over thousands of trials is what makes me a winning player.

While there is no one "correct" way to play poker, there is one universal truth on the felt: Winning at poker is much more fun than losing. With that in mind, I sincerely hope that the instructive hands presented in this book, paired with the tutelage in the *Little Green Book*, will make you a better player.

Throughout the hands presented here I ask the same question over and over again: "What would you do?" When you get to that question, you might want to stop and seriously consider your next move. (And don't cheat by reading ahead to see how I played it!) Rather than simply answering "raise" or "fold," try to come up with a full and rational explanation for your decision. Then the next time you get to the real table, try to do the same thing.

Now let's get straight to the tables—together—and explore some of the critical hands that have helped me take my game to the next level. I hope they will do the same for you!

PLAYER ATTRIBUTES

When I'm at the table, I'm constantly categorizing my opponents and trying to figure out how they play. By working hard and using that information, I can often make better, higher-quality decisions.

Are they beginners, likely focusing on the cards in front of them, or top pros using multilevel psychology to throw me off their scent? Do they play "no fold'em hold'em," or are they "rocks" who will wait patiently for a premium hand? Are they aggressive players who will bet into any empty space, or calling stations who will never, ever fold to a bluff? Have they recently won or lost a momentum-shifting pot? Are they on tilt?

Obviously there are many more factors to consider than the cards you've been dealt. Throughout the hands in this book, I have attempted to convey some of the most relevant information I've managed to absorb from my opponents. Please note that the stack size listed in the table diagrams is after players have posted blinds, antes, and acted as indicated.

CASH GAMES

Tournaments like the *World Series of Poker* (*WSOP*) or the *World Poker Tour* (*WPT*) may get all the headlines, but there are a lot of purists who believe that cash games represent the only "true" way to play poker. In a cash game, you can't get eliminated by a bad beat, at least as long as you have cash in your wallet. There aren't any artificial constraints like short stacks or increasing blinds and antes—the best strategies are the ones that most effectively separate your opponents from their money. Most important, especially to the pros who make their living at the game, the good players will eventually win, while the bad players will ultimately get their comeuppance.

Cash games are all about long-term results. The goal, therefore, is to make decisions that carry positive equity. In tournaments it's generally a bad idea to risk all of your chips in situations where you are only a slight favorite—get into two 55-45 "races," and odds are, you're going to lose one and find yourself stumbling for the exit. In a cash game, however, as long as you have a big enough bankroll, the statistically favorable play is always the best play. You'll still face your share of bad luck, but a player who consistently makes quality decisions will survive these short-term fluctuations and, over time, come out ahead. Hopefully far ahead. Very far ahead.

ALOHA, FULL HOUSE!

THE SITUATION: A loose, drunken nine-handed No Limit cash game on a Friday night at the Palms Casino, Las Vegas.

—— NO LIMIT HOLD'EM ——
Blinds $2/$5

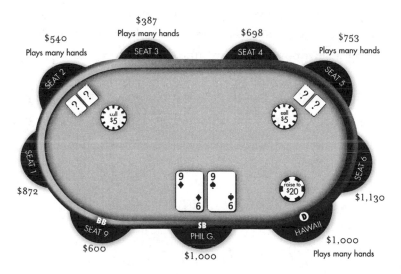

POT: $37   **TO CALL:** $18   **POT ODDS:** 2.1–1

I love playing pocket pairs in multiway pots. I'm either going to flop a set (or better) and have a chance to win a very big pot, or I'll miss and escape without doing too much damage to my stack.

The action gets to "Hawaii," a middle-aged guy wearing a bright floral-print button-up, in Seat 7. That wardrobe should be illegal, and it's more than moderately distracting. In keeping with the island theme, he's ordering piña coladas by the bucketful. He raises to $20.

At the moment, the pot isn't giving me favorable odds. . . . I'm only getting 2–1 to call, while the odds of my flopping a set or better are around 8–1 against. My implied odds, however, are excellent—if Hawaii turns out to have any kind of hand and I make my set, I'll have a very good shot of doubling up. I love that he has a grand in front of him.

I call the raise. So do Seats 2 and 5. There is $85 in the pot.

—— THE FLOP ——

Mahalo! I suppress the urge to break out and hula dance, though Kool and the Gang's "Celebration" starts echoing in my subconscious. Now the key is to figure out how to maximize the amount of money I stand to win. Do I bet out, or slowplay?

What would you do?

I begin my decision-making process by creating a mental image of how this hand is likely to play out. Hawaii, the preflop aggressor, seems likely to bet; I'm confident that I'll be able to separate him from some money. But I'm greedier than that: I want to trap the two players in the middle as well.

If Hawaii were on my immediate left, I'd probably check my hand, allow him to bet and hope that the two players in the middle call, then trap them all with a raise when the action returned to me. With Hawaii last to act, however, I'm going to have to trap the two players in the middle *before* the action gets to him. I'll make a small bet here, one that I hope one or two players in the middle can call, and pray that Hawaii can raise.

I bet $20. Seats 2 and 5 both call. Perfect! Hawaii raises to $150. Sucker! The plan worked to perfection! There is $295 in the pot, and it will cost me $w30 to call. As "Hannibal" Smith used to say to the A-Team, "I love it when a plan comes together!" Now, do I just call the bet here, or bring down the hammer with a raise?

What would you do?

I'm inclined to re-raise here for three reasons:

1. Hawaii's bet is probably large enough to scare off our other two opponents, so there's not much point in trying to keep them around much longer.

2. If Hawaii has a flush draw, say A♣K♣, he'll probably be willing to put all of his money into the pot right now. If he doesn't have a flush draw and another club comes on the turn, he might shut down.

3. If Hawaii is overplaying an overpair, as tourists wearing Hawaiian shirts to a casino are apt to do, say T-T, J-J, or Q-Q, and an overcard or flush card comes on the turn, it will be very difficult to extract all of his chips. If he has an overpair, I think it's very likely he'll push all-in against me right away.

I decide to re-raise and give him a chance to jump into molten lava.

I re-raise to $300. Seats 2 and 5 quickly fold. Hawaii doesn't hesitate: He pushes all-in. Luau time! I move my chips into the middle so fast that I burn skid marks into the felt. My somewhat dazed opponent turns over pocket queens, an overpair to the board. He's drawing slim to two outs. The turn and river rain harmless clubs, the K♣ and J♣. I scoop the pot with both hands.

"I put you on a flush draw," Hawaii comments

as he slurps the last of his drink and fishes for the cherry.

In retrospect it was a good thing I made my move when I did—the turn probably would have slowed him down. In comparison to the grand I won from the big fish, the extra $40 I won by betting right out seems insignificant. But it's $40 I wouldn't have won had I just checked the flop, and it will come in handy when Antonio "Mr. Bottle Service" Esfandiari and I meet up for drinks at the Ghost Bar in a few hours. I've been out with that guy about thirty times, and I've never left a bar without parting with at least $500. Antonio is a one-man bankroll wrecking machine at and away from the tables.

❧ KEY ANALYSIS ❧

Pocket pairs possess a lot of implied value, especially in multiway pots, where they present you with a chance to win a lot or lose a little. When you are lucky enough to flop a monster hand, take a minute to figure out how the action is likely to play out . . . and how you can maximize your winnings. Poker isn't about winning pots: It's about winning as much money as you possibly can on the hands you decide to play.

A WEIRD DRAW

THE SITUATION: Midnight in a loose seven-handed No Limit Hold'em game at the Borgata in Atlantic City, New Jersey.

——NO LIMIT HOLD'EM CASH GAME——
Blinds $2/$5

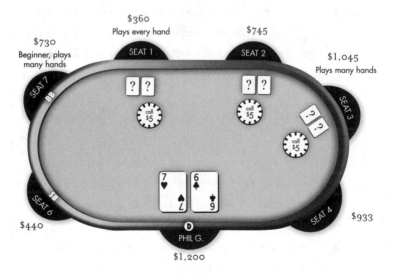

POT: $22   **TO CALL:** $5   **POT ODDS:** 4.4–1

Decisions, decisions. Seven-six offsuit isn't a great hand, but I'm in position with excellent pot odds and no one has shown any kind of strength here. This feels like a "family pot" situation.

What would you do?

If this were the middle or late stages of a tournament, I'd give serious thought to raising here against a group of loose limpers. But in a loose "no fold'em hold'em" game like this, that play never works. The real value in this hand comes from the implied odds and my position—if I can flop a great hand, I will have a chance to win a big pot.

Before I limp in, however, I will consider the players left to act, behind me: Are any of them likely to make the "raise the limpers" play I was just considering? In this case neither player has demonstrated much aggression or skill, so the answer is probably no. If one of them does raise, though, I'm done with this hand.

I call $5 from the button. The small blind tosses in three bucks to complete the blind, and the big blind checks. There are six players and $30 in the pot.

——THE FLOP——

This is a dangerous flop for me. I perform a bit of quick mental calculus:

"Dumb" end of a straight draw
+ A very weak flush draw
+ 5 loose opponents
—————————————————————————————
= A perfect opportunity for me to lose a lot of money

All five players check to me. Should I bet or check? What would you do?

I know, I said this was a dangerous flop. But I can't just leave that money lying there in the middle with all the weakness on display, can I?

When I flop a draw in position against many opponents and it gets checked around to me, I'll often just check and take a free look at the turn card. In this situation, however, I really don't have that much of a draw . . . or, better said, I have several draws that I might not want to make.

First let's look at the kinds of hands that my opponents were likely to limp in with: weak aces, medium pocket pairs, suited cards and/or connectors.

A heart will make me a flush, but will give a better flush to anyone who has the T♥ or better. A ten will make me a straight but will make a bigger straight for someone holding Q-J or even J-7. The only card that I'd really like to see is a five that isn't a heart—that's three "clean" outs, giving me about a 6% chance of feeling secure about my hand on the turn. There is also a pretty good chance that I'm already drawing dead and someone flopped the flush and decided to slowplay.

If I want this pot, I'm better off taking a stab at it now. Betting between half and three quarters of the pot makes it "incorrect" for anyone to call me with a small flush or straight draw. I'm using the "scare" quotes here because anyone who knew what I actually had would not only likely be correct in calling but would probably race me to get his chips in the middle. Fortunately, poker isn't played with the hole cards exposed.*

I bet $15, half the pot. Everyone folds except the big blind, who calls. There is $60 in the pot.

That wasn't a terrible result—only the worst player at the table stands between me and taking this pot. If someone put a gun to my head and forced me to guess at his hand, I'd say that he was holding the A♥ with a weak kicker.

——THE TURN——

---

* There is only one exception, and he's a "friend" to the poker world. Kasey "Flop" Thompson has been known to play $400/$800 Limit Hold'em while exposing both of his hole cards for the entirety of the hand. Every hand. Kasey is very popular in the casinos, as you might expect.

Not a bad card for me. If my opponent thought I had top pair, then he has to think my hand just got a lot better. If, as I suspect is the case, he's paying less attention to me than he is to his chances of catching a card, well, that probably wasn't the card he was waiting for.

The big blind checks to me. What would you do?

While I almost definitely do not have the best hand right now, my opponent doesn't know that. I want him to think that I'm in front, and that the turn card helped me.

How would I play this hand if the 9♦ really had helped me? I'd probably try to take down the pot right here and now with a good-size bet.

I fire the second bullet and bet $40. The big blind calls very quickly. There is $140 in the pot. He has to have some sort of flush draw, probably the nut flush draw.

——THE RIVER——

Again, a good card for me . . . or at least the hand I'm trying to represent. If the big blind was on the nut flush draw or a straight draw of some sort, he just missed.

He checks to me. It's decision time again. Fire the

third bullet and bet, or just give up the hand? What would you do?

This one's a no-brainer. . . . It's incredibly unlikely that my seven-high will win a showdown. Either I trust my read—he's on a draw and missed—or I concede the pot.

I'm not going to concede the pot. If he's been slow-playing a monster, I'm about to find out. . . . I cock the gun, gather my courage, and bet $70. That $70 is exactly the same bet I'd make if I had flopped the flush or turned trip nines. My betting has been consistent throughout the hand. The big blind grumbles something about his bad luck, flashes the A♥, and folds his hand.

"Lucky flop for me," I say, adding his chips to mine. For future hands I note that this player is a "check-caller" and plays very passively.

❧ KEY ANALYSIS ❧

A scary board can be your greatest ally if you can use it to narrow down the range of hands your opponent(s) might be playing and tell a consistent story with your bets.

MIND GAMES

THE SITUATION: Friday afternoon, a six-handed cash game on FullTiltPoker.com featuring very aggressive players.

——NO LIMIT HOLD'EM CASH GAME——
Blinds $5/$10

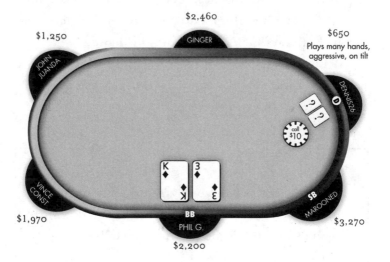

POT: $25   **TO CALL:** $0

Dennis26 and I have been going round and round. I've taken him for about $1,200 in the last ten minutes, and if his chat is any indication, he's clearly steaming.

This has been an extremely aggressive table, so it comes as a bit of a surprise when I get a free look at the flop from the big blind. I give no thought at all to raising. With him on mega-tilt there is no way I can get him to fold, and I'll be out of position for the rest of the hand. I'm mildly surprised he didn't "Auto-Raise" on his button. Maybe, just maybe, he's trying to set some sort of trap. Then again, maybe he's just steaming.

I check. There is $25 in the pot.

——THE FLOP——

This is obviously a great flop for me. Should I bet or check?

What would you do?

There are a couple of ways to play this hand:

1. Bet right out and hope to get raised.
2. Check, hope he tries to use his position and bets, then check-raise (or go for the super-slowplay-check-call play.)

Against a normal, non-tilting opponent I'd probably just bet right out and hope he could call me. Against

Dennis26, I feel very confident that I should let him hang himself. I decide to check.

When the board is paired, the chance that someone actually "caught a piece" of the flop is much lower. In these situations the first person to bet at the pot often wins. Dennis26 knows this. As on tilt as he is, there is no way he'll be able to resist making a bet here.

I check, and Dennis26 quickly bets the pot, $25. With $50 in the pot the action is on me. Calling or check-raising are my two options; folding is clearly not a possibility unless my hand slips off my mouse or my Internet connection fails.

What would you do?

Well, if I check-raise, the hand is likely to be over. Even a supertilter like Dennis26 is unlikely to risk more chips facing a check-raise. It has to be a better idea to continue the ruse, represent a hand like a pair of fives, and just call.

I call. The pot now has $75 in it.

——THE TURN——

I formed a plan, and the turn card doesn't change much. I'm still going to give him a chance to hang himself. Here's a little more rope, Dennis: I check.

Dennis26 makes it $125, an overbet. There is $200 in the pot. It looks like my little strategy paid off: That overbet is W-E-A-K. I definitely have him. I consider my choices carefully: Drop the hammer with a raise, or continue my slowplay?

What would you do?

I'm going for the maximum—I'm going to give him a chance to tilt bluff off the rest of his money on the river. I call the $125, bringing the pot to a nice $325.

——THE RIVER——

An innocent-looking card. I have two options: check and hope to elicit another bluff, or bet right out and hope to get called by his piece-of-cheese hand.

What would you do?

Against a guy tilting like this, either play could get the money. Because of his state of mind, I think there are a lot more hands that he will bluff with than hands that he'll be happy to showdown and hope to win on merit. With that in mind I go for the ultimate slowplay and check yet again.

He takes the bait and bets $325. He has just $175

remaining. I can check-raise him all-in, or I can just call the $325.

What would you do?

Against a rational player the call would be clear. Raising all-in with this medium-strength hand on the river would be bad business: He'd call me only if he could beat me. But against this yahoo, rationality has left the building. I firmly expect him to pay me off with any pair in his hand. I raise him all-in.

Maybe I'm imagining things, but it looks like there is steam coming out of the ears of his avatar—which is, appropriately enough, a donkey. The seconds tick away. Finally he calls and shows A-5, not to mention a zero balance. I quickly disable observer chat to avoid what I'm sure is a long stream of expletives not fit for print.

❖ KEY ANALYSIS ❖

Your opponent's state of mind can greatly affect how you play a hand. While the cards are important, understanding the motivations and weaknesses of your opponents is far more critical. Also, keep an eye out for Dennis26—he's probably still on tilt.

RUSTY NAILS

THE SITUATION: A low-stakes cash game, Tuesday, four a.m., Mandalay Bay poker room.

——NO LIMIT HOLD'EM——
Blinds $2/$5

POT: $20   TO CALL: $10   POT ODDS: 2–1

I'll leave it as an exercise for the reader to figure out why I'm at Mandalay Bay at four a.m. on a Tuesday playing

$2/$5 No Limit. In all honesty, I can't remember myself.

"I raise," slurs the guy in the small blind. Familiar words, as he's been repeating them all night in between sips of the half-dozen Rusty Nails (a Tiltboy favorite consisting of equal parts Scotch and Drambuie). Do I call the drunk guy, raise, or fold?

What would you do?

A-T is a pretty good hand heads-up, and I'm in position. I don't think there's any chance that a raise is going to get him to lay his hand down, but I have some compelling reasons for upping the bet here: I think I have the best hand, I can take control of the betting, and there's at least a remote possibility that he'll pass out (thus giving me the pot) before the action gets back to him.

"Re-raise to $40," I say, as I very slowly count out eight $5 chips and slide them into the middle.

"What the heck, Philly. Let's see a fthlop."

There is $80 in the pot. I wipe a bit of his spittle off my chin as the dealer lays the first three cards on the table. . . .

——THE FLOP——

28

"I check," he says in a way that makes "check" sound like a two-syllable word.

This was a good flop for me: I have top pair, the board texture isn't particularly threatening, and I have a backdoor flush to a draw. Make that a draw to a flush—am I tired, or is drunkenness contagious? In any case a bet seems like the clear-cut action.

What would you do?

A bet of around half the pot seems right to me. "Forty-five dollars," I say, making the pot $125.

"Philly, Philly, Philly, Bananamana-pho-philly . . . ," he sings, serenading no one in particular. "I call."

With $170 sitting between us, this has suddenly turned into a real pot.

——THE TURN——

Rusty Nail *cha-hecks* to me again. I take a second to work through my options. This has become a substantial pot, and I wouldn't mind taking it down now.

What could he have? Just about anything. A weak ace, a medium pocket pair. Hell, he could even have J-4. Or he could just be drunk.

Still, one pair isn't that great a hand. But I still have top pair with a decent kicker, and now I have a flush draw.

What would you do?

Without particular conviction I bet $100. He waves at the pot. "I'm awllllllll-in."

I'm about to puke. It suddenly dawns on me that maybe he raised with a legitimate hand. "Count it," I ask the dealer, mostly to buy more time. I already know that his bet is going to put me all-in.

It isn't clear that another ace or ten will give me a winner. The only clear road to victory is a flush.

"Another $131 to call," says the dealer. I look down at my own stack, which has been whittled down to $100.

This is a simple math problem, something Rusty Nail would have no chance of doing right now:

Step 1: Count my outs. I know I have nine outs, as any heart will make a flush. There may be other outs that will make me a winning hand, but because I could be up against two pair or a set already, I won't count them.

Step 2: Use the Rule of Two. 9 outs x 2 = an 18% chance of making my flush on the river.

Step 3: Find my Break Even Percentage. There is $470 currently in the pot. If I call with my last $100, the pot will contain $570. My $100 will represent

$100/$570 of the pot, or 17.5%. I need a 17.5%

chance or better to win in order to justify a call.

Step 4: Make a winning decision.

Equity decisions don't get too much closer than this one. If I'm beat right now and need to make a flush to win, it really doesn't matter from an equity perspective if I call or fold—my long-term results should be the same. But there is at least a small chance that Rusty Nail has lost what little brain function he has remaining and I'm ahead, in which case that entire pot-odds Rule of Two exercise was wasted energy. The chance that I'm already holding the best hand turns a close decision into a statistically profitable one.

I call. Rusty turns over A-J, good for top two pair. I need a heart to win.

The river is the 2♣. No rabbit in this hat.

"I had you DOM-inated," he says as he gathers the rest of my chips. The sad truth is, he's right.

❖ KEY ANALYSIS ❖

Use the mathematics of poker to make positive equity decisions. Be careful when playing hands that are easily dominated—even drunks can play top two pair effectively!

FLASHBACK

THE SITUATION: Online at FullTiltPoker.com and playing four different No Limit Hold'em cash games at the same time. Yes, its possible. Not recommended, but possible.

——NO LIMIT HOLD'EM——
Blinds $2/$5

POT: $7   **TO CALL**: $3   **POT ODDS**: 2.3–1

Sunday morning and I'm jacked up on coffee. I should be working on this book, but instead I have four different No Limit Hold'em tables on my screen. I'm moving and tapping my mouse to the beat of an old Nirvana song.

I'm trying to remember the last time I heard the song, when a caffeine-spasm literally jerks me back into reality. Everyone folds to me in the small blind. My hand twitches, I click the "Raise Min" button instead of the "Fold" button, and suddenly I've upped the bet to $10 from the small blind. The big blind calls with frightening speed.

I look at the hand that I've decided to play: J♥2♥. "Cavalier mini-raise, Phil," sneers my inner poker critic. Jack-two is a terrible hand, and being suited isn't as valuable as people think it is.

——THE FLOP——

"I am a poker genius!" I shout at the plant in the corner of the room. "I am going to milk this hand for— oh, *now* I remember when I last heard this song!"

Flash back to 1992 . . .

I'm sitting at a poker table at the Garden City Casino in San Jose, California. I have a lot more hair. I've got a Walkman on, listening to a cassette tape my girlfriend made me.* Some guy named Kurt Cobain is singing a song about, if I'm understanding the words correctly, *stupid* being contagious.

The action gets folded around to me in the small blind, where I find J♥2♥. "Sweet! It's suited!" The guy on my left taps me on the shoulder. I lift a headphone off my ear.

"You know you're talking out loud," he says.

"Well, maybe I was bluffing," I respond sheepishly. "I raise."

The guy shakes his head at me as he raises to $30. "If poker ever gets popular with the kids, we're all doomed," he says. I call the $30 because, after all, I'm suited!

The flop comes K♥T♥3♥. I lean backward in my chair, trying to look nonchalant. Time to slowplay. "I check."

The guy grins at me and raps the table. The dealer burns a card and lays down the turn. It's the 9♥. "I bet—," I start to say, but before I can finish, he's tossed two black aces faceup into the muck.

"Shoulda bet the flop, kid," he mutters. "You mighta got all my chips."

---

* If you're under twenty-five, you might have to ask your parents about "cassettes."

Flash forward to 2006 . . .

"Man, was I an idiot back then," I explain to the plant. "Not only did I overvalue suitedness, but I didn't bet the flop and lost all my action when the fourth heart hit the turn. Oh yeah, and I slouched back in my chair when I made a hand—a definite tell."

"I need water," replies the plant. I make a mental note to reduce the amount of caffeine in my diet, and I look at my cards again. I still have J♥2♥, and the board is still A♥9♥8♥.

What would you do?

"Time for a bet," I say. I choose a slight overbet of the pot, $30, and really hope that the big blind hit an ace. No slowplay here. If he doesn't have an ace, I'm not really likely to win much more money. If he does have an ace, all the money is likely to go into the pot.

He takes just a second before raising me to $90. Should I slowplay and just call the $90, or move all-in?

What would you do?

Moving all-in is clearly my best move. I am almost certain I have the best hand, and my opponent is definitely pot committed.

I move all-in in a flash, and it's clear by the ticking

clock that he's not happy. Just before his time is about to run out, he calls and shows A♦J♣.

"He's drawing dead!" I yell at the plant. When the virtual dealer burns and turns the Q♥, I know I've played this hand exactly right: That heart on the turn definitely would have shut down my action had I slowplayed.

❖ KEY ANALYSIS ❖

Suitedness only adds a couple of percentage points to your winning percentage—you're only going to flop a flush about one time in 119. When you do, however, the best play is usually to bet out and hope you are called or raised; the action can very easily dry up later in the hand.

THE RIVER APU

THE SITUATION: A No Limit Hold'em cash game at Hank Azaria's house in Hollywood.

Blinds $5/$10

$1,000 AJAY
$700 BRIAN
$1,200 RUDD
$800 MATTHEW
$1,900 NEWMAN
BB HANK $970
SB PHIL G. $940
D SEAT 6 $1,100

POT: $15   **TO CALL:** $5   **POT ODDS:** 3–1

When everyone folds to me in the small blind, my
A-9 suited isn't a powerhouse, but it stands to be the best
right now. Given that I'll be out of position against my
host, Hank Azaria—a very nice guy (and a brilliant actor)
who happens to be a loose-aggressive poker player—I'd
rather take down this pot before the flop. I'll stick to the
upper end of my spectrum of small blind raises, about
three-and-a-half times the big blind.

I raise to $35. Hank quickly says "call" in the voice of Apu, one of the many characters he "voices" for *The Simpsons*. I love it when he does that—the voice, that is, not calling me when I'm out of position. There is $70 in the pot.

——THE FLOP——

Hank is a very capable player, and I know he loves to play in position. This flop is a little dangerous because many of the hands that Hank might call with in this spot "connect" with the J-9.

What would you do?

My middle pair of nines is probably the best hand right now, and if Hank has played something like T-8, Q-T, K-Q, or K-T, I need to protect my hand (which isn't very likely to improve) against any potential draws. In fact, I want to take the pot right now. A pot-size bet will hopefully do the trick.

I bet $70. Hank calls very quickly, no voice this time. There is $210 in the pot.

The "quick call" is often a sign that an opponent is on a draw. With no flush on the board my best guess is Q-T or T-8. I really don't think he'd call my pot-size bet with only a gut-shot straight draw, although Hank is crafty and unpredictable enough to do just about anything.

──THE TURN──

This is both a good and a bad card for me. I've picked up a flush draw, but if he is playing Q-8 or K-Q, he's just moved ahead of me. I'm faced with a tough decision.

What would you do?

I hate to give up control of the betting, but when a scare card like this hits the turn, that is often the right play.

I check. Hank fires $150 into the middle, bringing the pot to a total of $360.

This is an interesting spot, and one that calls for some math:

Step 1: I count my outs. I know I have nine outs to the nut flush. If my read is correct, and he has a hand like Q-T or T-8, then I also have three aces and two nines in the deck that will help me, a total of fourteen outs in all. He may have a straight, however. . . . I'm going to compensate by shaving my chances down to twelve outs.

Step 2: Use the Rule of Two. With twelve outs, the Rule of Two tells me that I have about a 24% chance of making a winning hand on the river.

Step 3: Calculate my pot odds and Break Even Percentage. I'm asked to call $150 to win $360, so I'm getting

39

2.4–1 on my money. My Break Even Percentage is
1 ÷ (2.4+1), or about 29%. I need a 29% chance to
win the hand to justify a call.

Clearly I'm not getting the right pot odds to call,
but I know I'm getting the right *implied* pot odds. If I make
the flush on the river, I'll definitely be able to extract
some money from Apu.

It's close, but I call. The pot swells to $510.

——THE RIVER——

Hi-ya! I've made my nut flush. While I silently
congratulate myself for being lucky at the right time, my
mind does cartwheels as I try to figure out how to separate
my friend from as much money as I can. I have to decide
between betting for value and trying for a check-raise.

What would you do?

I go through my mental checklist:

♣ Is the river a scary card for my opponent? A little.
While my play so far hasn't necessarily been consistent
with a flush draw, the flush is out there. That's one
vote for betting out.

♣ Was he on a draw that missed? Yes, if he had Q-T or Q-J; no, if he had a straight, two pair, or a set. He'll certainly bet a straight, and he'll probably bet a set as well. He is very likely to check all hands that are one or two pair—Hank doesn't like to bet medium-strength hands on the river, because he's a good player.

♣ Is he very aggressive? Yes, very. One vote for the check-raise.

♣ Does he think he has the best hand? If he has a straight, most definitely. It will be very difficult for him to put me on a runner-runner flush.

♣ Can he afford to make a bet if I check? There is $510 in the middle; he has nearly $800 in his stack. That's a definite yes, and another vote for check-raising.

♣ Is he likely to pay off a check-raise? If he has a straight, yes; otherwise, no. That's a big vote not only for betting out but for overbetting the pot.

♣ Have I already check-raised on this hand? No. If I had, I definitely wouldn't check-raise again. One vote for check-raise.

All in all, I think it's a mighty close decision between betting and check-raising. I could really go either way. I flip a coin in my head. It comes up heads. I bet out $150, a number I think he can call.

He re-raises me all-in. I call so fast that I frighten myself.

Holding his hands to his face and pulling out his best Mr. Bill voice, Hank says, "Oh no, Mr. Phil!" He turns over Q♠8♠ for a second-best straight.

This was an odd outcome when you think about it in retrospect. If I had gone for the check-raise, he probably would have made a small value bet, hoping to get paid off for his straight. My check-raise might have given him a reason to get away from his hand, although it would have been very difficult to lay down a straight.

❧ KEY ANALYSIS ❧

The choice between betting and check-raising on the river is often a close decision. In most cases you're better off erring on the side of betting.

MATH GENIUS

THE SITUATION: An aggressive No Limit Wednesday-morning cash game at the Bellagio.

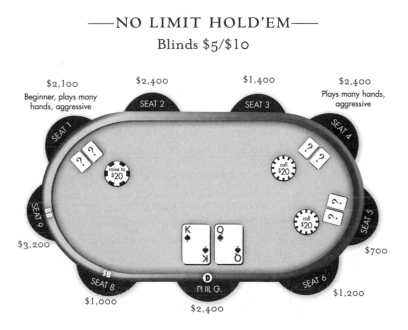

—NO LIMIT HOLD'EM—
Blinds $5/$10

POT: $75   **TO CALL:** $20   **POT ODDS:** 3.8–1

After a breakfast business meeting at the Bellagio, I decide to drop by the poker room to check out the action. I find an empty seat shortly after eleven a.m., and take a moment to study my opponents. They look well-rested and competent. At least half of them look to be cash-game pros: true grinders. There's a second where I consider a quick escape, until I remember that I am a pro and not supposed to be afraid of these kinds of players.

"Hey, I'll just play a few rounds," I say as I pull all the cash out of my pocket and buy a few racks of chips.

A player I know to be loose and aggressive makes the minimum raise under the gun. Two players call. My K-Q suited is an easily dominated hand, but in a multiway pot I can treat it more like a suited connector than two big cards. Given my superior position, folding for only $20 seems out of the question. I can raise or call.

What would you do?

When confronted with a decision at the poker table, I like to start by considering the most aggressive option. The first question I ask myself is this: "Should I raise?"

Two of the three players who have entered the pot are loose-aggressive players who aren't afraid to push all of their chips into the middle with big aces (A-K, A-Q) or pocket pairs. If I were certain I had the best hand, I would probably raise, but I don't think that's the case here. I'd rather not raise and get re-raised, as I'd likely be an underdog to whatever cards the re-raiser was holding.

I call the $20. Both blinds fold. There is $95 in the pot.

——THE FLOP——

A decent but not great flop for me. Obviously, I don't have anything more than high cards. A ten will give me a nut straight, and there's always the possibility of catching runner-runner spades to make a flush. That'll happen about 5% of the time.

On the other hand I'm not sure that a king or queen will help me, as they create all kinds of straight and two pair possibilities for the hands I'm likely to be facing: Q-T, K-T, Q-J, K-J, and so on. If there's any significant action in front of me, I'll probably fold.

Everyone checks to me.

This is an interesting development. If I were certain that the checks represented weakness, I wouldn't hesitate to bet here. The board texture is very coordinated, however, and it's doubtful, if not impossible, that the board missed all three of my opponents.

What would you do? Bet and try to take the pot, or check and take a look at the turn card?

Someone could definitely be slowplaying a set or a

pat straight. Because no one bet, I now have unlimited odds to draw at a nut straight, whereas if I bet and get check-raised, I'm almost certainly going to have to throw my hand away. I'm happy to check here and take a free shot at spiking a ten on the turn.

——THE TURN——

No miracle ten, but the A♠ does add the nut flush draw to my list of dream outcomes.

The preflop raiser leads out with a $120 bet. The loose-aggressive caller calls. There is $335 in the pot, and it will cost me $120 to call.

Things are heating up.... Were one or both of them slowplaying big hands? Did the ace help both players? How could both of them feel so good about their hands when I know neither has the king or queen of spades?

The ace was an especially good card for me, as it ensures that my flush, should I get there, will be the best. It doesn't hurt my straight possibilities either. With nine flush outs and another three tens in the deck (I've already counted the fourth ten with the spades), I have twelve outs to a nut hand.

Well, maybe not. If one of these guys does have a set, then I certainly don't want to see the J♠ or 7♠, which will create a full house (or better) for the lucky player. I will err on the conservative side here and estimate eleven clean outs.

Step 1: Count the outs. . . . I've done this, and I'm guessing eleven.

Step 2: Use the Rule of Two. I calculate that I have about a 22% chance of making my hand on the river. 11 x 2 = 22%.

Step 3: Figure out my Break Even Percentage (BEP). The pot is offering me odds of $335/$120, or 2.8–1. My BEP is 1 ÷ (2.8 + 1), or about 26%.

I need a 26% chance to win to justify calling. I'm not getting the correct odds to continue with the hand . . . right now. But could my *implied odds* justify a call? How much money will I have to extract from my opponents on the river if I make my winning hand to make calling now a profitable decision?

I visualize how big the pot will have to be if I

make my hand in order to justify calling. Here if I can extract just another $90 or $100 from my opponent on the river if I make my winning hand, then my call after the turn will have been profitable. Given the action on this hand, that seems like a pretty reasonable assumption.

Keep in mind that the only thing that makes this a "safe" play for me is that I'm on the button. A call from me closes out the betting, so I won't be forced to invest any additional money into this pot. Were there players still to act after me, I'd almost definitely fold here, as the possibility of a raise—and even a re-raise from one of the early position players—would throw all of this math out the window.

All in all, I think this is a really close decision between calling and folding. In a tournament, where chips are a limited commodity, I would almost certainly fold. In a cash game against aggressive players with deep stacks who might be more willing to pay off a big bet if I make my hand, I can afford to take on a little more risk.

I call $120. There is $455 in the pot. "Spade, Spade, Spade," I think as the dealer reveals the river card. . . .

Spade . . . but not the "clean" spade I was looking for. My worst suspicions get confirmed when the preflop raiser massively overbets the pot and pushes all-in for nearly $2,000. The loose-aggressive caller calls the big overbet instantly.

Ugh. If there's any silver lining at all to this situation, it's that I'm seated at the poker table, far away from any sharp objects.

Can I really lay down the nut flush? Let me consider some of the factors:

♥ Is my opponent's play (or, in this case, opponents' play) consistent with what I know about them? Yes. Either could have been hoping to check-raise on the flop with a set, so either could have a full house or better.

♥ Am I really pot committed? No. I have invested only $140 into this pot. The hand hasn't done too much damage thus far.

♥ Do my opponents respect my play? Who knows? Maybe a better question is, "Could both of them really *dis*respect my play enough to create this kind of action?" That seems unlikely, especially given that there's at least a small possibility that the twenty seconds or so it took me to do all of the math on the turn tipped them off to my flush draw.

♥ Have I been forced off good hands recently? No, I haven't been pushed around at all.

♥ Can my opponent(s) afford to be making a mistake? Maybe in a broad sense—if they're wealthy enough, they can always reach back into their wallets—but in terms of the money in play on the table, they are both putting it all on the line.

What would you do?

I take one last peek—okay, maybe two last peeks—at my cards and toss them into the muck.

The pain doesn't last long: The preflop raiser turns over pocket jacks for quads, more than enough to beat the loose-aggressive caller, who rubs his T-6 of spades, a flush, so hard that I'm afraid they might catch fire. I'm a little bit lighter in the pocket but happy to have avoided a disaster. My hand would have been so much more difficult to lay down had my opponent bet, say, $450 instead of moving all-in.

More good news: The loose-aggressive caller is reaching into his wallet for another stack of hundreds. The implied tilt odds are going to be juicy. Real juicy. I call and cancel my afternoon appointments—I'm going to be right here, rubbing the felt.

❧ K E Y   A N A L Y S I S ❧

When the pot odds are not in your favor, don't forget to consider the implied odds; very often you won't have to extract much money from your opponents on the river to justify a call on the turn. And when you're using the Rules of Four and Two, make sure that you take the board texture into account—not every out is an out you want to see.

TILTING LENNIE

THE SITUATION: The Tiltboy home game, Palo Alto, California. Thursday, two a.m.

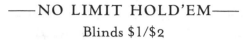

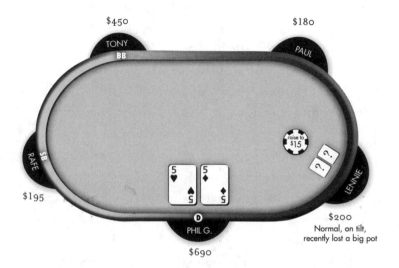

$450 $180
TONY   PAUL
BB

raise to $15

? ?

$SB
RAFE   LENNIE

$195

D

PHIL G.

$200
Normal, on tilt,
recently lost a big pot

$690

POT: $18   **TO CALL:** $15   **POT ODDS:** 1.2–1

You've got to feel sorry for Lennie: He is known as the unluckiest guy we know, and he's really living up to his reputation. He's gone broke twice in the last twenty minutes after getting it all-in before the flop with A-A against A-K. He's steaming.

I'm sympathetic . . . to a point. Whatever I'm feeling falls far short of anything resembling mercy. I want to bury my friend. Sad? Perhaps. But true.

Is pocket fives, colloquially known as "presto," the right hand to take against this Tiltboy?

What would you do?

His raise here may very well be legitimate, but it could also be a steam/tilt raise. I could come over the top with a re-raise, but I think it's more effective to just call in position.

I call $15. Tony and Rafe fold. We're heads-up with $33 in the pot.

——THE FLOP——

Lennie leads out with a weak-looking $10 bet. There is $43 in the pot, and it will cost me $10 to call.

A bet that small generally means one of two things:

1. He has a hand like pocket queens or jacks and is afraid I have an ace.
2. He has a hand like A-A or A-K and is trying to lure me into a trap.

What would you do?

It might be time for a little implied tilt raise. If I raise and get him to fold Q-Q or J-J, he'll almost certainly show his hand. I'll, of course, show my hand. Then he'll bust a gasket, rebuy, and continue to spew money like a broken cash machine. If I happen to catch him with a big hand, say A-K, I'll have six outs (four for the straight and two to make a set) to send him to Stanford Hospital's psych ward. I know he's got a nice little paycheck for $1,000 in his wallet—if I can put another bad beat on him here, we might just see some serious money hit the table.

Hey, what are friends for, right? I raise him all-in and he calls in a shot, while turning over yet another set of aces. Ouch.

"That's okay," I say in my best (but still terrible) John Malkovich-from-*Rounders* impersonation. "I pay you with your own money." Everyone seems to know what's coming next, and it's not going to be pretty.

Rafe burns and turns and puts a six on the board. Lennie sighs, and in a resigned voice says: "Come on, I know it's coming, deal the damn three on the river and get it over with."

Well, he asked for it. A beautiful (from my perspective, anyway) three hits the river. Lennie ships his chips on over. More important, he takes out the $1,000 check. "Can we raise the table limit, guys?" he asks.

As his best friends, we're happy to oblige.

❈ KEY ANALYSIS ❈

Do not underestimate the power of implied tilt odds. You can at times take the worst of it if a monster suckout will open a fire hose of angry tilting money.

I'M NOT BLUFFING

THE SITUATION: A No Limit cash game at the Palms Casino Resort in Las Vegas, the day before the fourth-season taping of *Celebrity Poker Showdown*.

—NO LIMIT HOLD'EM—
Blinds $2/$5

$564

Plays many hands,
somewhat passive

$424

$664

SEAT 6

SEAT 7

$348

D

SEAT 5

JOSH MALINA

SB

SEAT 4

BB

SEAT 9

$110

$450

SEAT 3

PHIL G.

SEAT 1

$440

$645

$280

POT: $7   **TO CALL:** $5   **POT ODDS:** 1.4–1

Everyone is psyched to be back on set for the fourth
season of *Celebrity Poker Showdown*. Shooting doesn't start
until tomorrow, however, and I'm checked in to the Palms
hotel with nothing to do for the rest of the evening . . .
until my good friend Josh Malina calls and asks if I want to
head down to the poker room. Josh, who created *Celebrity
Poker Showdown* (and recruited me!) with his friend Andrew

Hill Newman, is a very, very good player who made a living at the game before landing acting gigs on *Sports Night* and *The West Wing*. I owe him quite a bit for the opportunity he gave me to break into television, but when we're at the table together, it's war. There are few people in the world I enjoy beating more than Josh. I'm sure he'd say the same thing about me.

Josh and I both buy in for $500, and after just a round of play, we're both slightly ahead. Now I've picked up A-K offsuit in early position and decide to make my standard raise of three times the size of the big blind.

I raise to $15. Everyone folds to Josh, who is in the small blind. If Josh has a weakness, he tends to play a loose-passive game from the blinds. He calls my raise; the big blind folds. I'm up against a good friend with a great hand, and I'm in position. Perfect!

There is $35 in the pot.

——THE FLOP——

Josh checks to me. I remember that Josh will nearly always go for a check-raise in this situation with a monster top pair, but I'm not sure if that should dissuade me from the nearly obligatory continuation bet.

What would you do? Check and hope to get him to make a big mistake on the turn, or bet here to protect your top pair?

Given that I have a powerhouse hand that isn't likely to improve, I think betting here is clear. If I get check-raised, I might have to reevaluate, but a continuation bet is nearly always the right play in this spot.

I decide on a bet of $20, a little more than half the pot. Josh ponders a moment, and then calls. There is $75 in the pot.

—THE TURN—

That turn card looks like a blank. Unless Josh is playing A-2, a rather unlikely scenario, I'm probably still in the lead. Josh checks, and I'm faced with another decision: Bet again, or go for a trap and check.

What would you do?

Josh could be slowplaying, but his penchant for check-raising after the flop with any really good hand leads me to believe I still have the best hand. My "book" on Josh suggests that he's playing something like K-Q or an ace with a mediocre kicker, and that he thinks I'm bluffing. He's playing passively in the hopes that I'll bluff off even more of my chips. The only hitch in his plan is that I'm *not* bluffing, and I think I can make him pay a price for his passivity.

I could make a huge bet to take down the pot now, but if Josh does have an ace with a weak kicker, I want him to call—he has only three outs to improve his hand. The Rule of Two tells me that against an ace with a weaker kicker than mine, there is about a 94% chance I'll still be ahead on the river. I think I can make a value bet here that he can call. Since no flush draws are possible, $50 into the $75 pot seems about right to me.

I bet $50. Josh calls with what appears like defiance. There is $175 in the pot.

——THE RIVER——

There's virtually no way Josh called my bets on the flop and turn with just a pair of sevens, so I'm nearly certain that I still have the best hand. When Josh checks to me yet again, it is time for maximum extraction.

How much would you bet?

As I said before, it seems as if Josh is trying to let me "bluff" off my chips. With the board paired Josh will probably call a bet with any weak ace, figuring that his worst-case scenario is a split pot with aces and sevens with a queen kicker. But as Scotty Nguyen might say, "Queen kicker no good!" If he's going to call me with a weak ace (or even a queen), I want it to hurt.

How much would you bet?

After deliberating I decide on $150, a bet big enough to suggest that I'm bluffing or trying to get him to throw away a hand that's tied with mine.

Josh shakes his head. I'm suddenly worried that I bet too much. "I really hope you didn't wake up with ace-king," he says. "But I know you, Phil, and you're more than capable of firing that third bullet. You'd love to run me out of this pot. . . . I call."

I try not to look too smug as I turn over my ace-king, but I'm not as good an actor as Josh is. Not that I'd mind seeing him go on tilt. . . .

"Nice hand, sir," he says, tossing his cards into the muck. Two minutes later a production assistant summons Josh to a very important meeting, saving him from tilting off any more money to me. I spot Dennis Rodman eyeing Josh's vacated seat. I can't get that lucky, can I?

❖ KEY ANALYSIS ❖

If your opponent (incorrectly) thinks you're bluffing, you can often get away with a much bigger value bet than you'd normally make. Make him pay a dear price to play "sheriff" against you.

GOING TO WAR WITH THE UNABOMBER

THE SITUATION: A high-stakes No Limit Hold'em game against several top pros. We've all just busted out of the $10,000 buy-in tournament during the second day at the *World Series of Poker* Circuit event in New Orleans.

— NO LIMIT HOLD'EM —
Blinds $25/$50

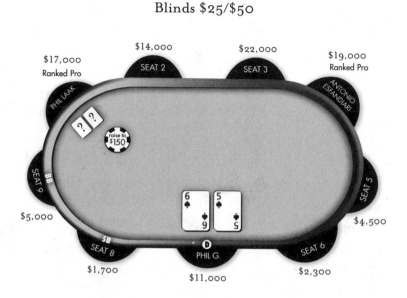

POT: $225   **TO CALL:** $150   **POT ODDS:** 1.5–1

I'm still steaming after busting out of a major $10,000 buy-in event with a completely boneheaded play. When will I learn to stop bluffing players who are incapable of folding? I've landed in a cash game that, despite the presence of a couple of top pros, looks pretty juicy, and I do my best to clear my head for the task at hand. I want to get some of that buy-in back!

Playing hands from early position is always tricky business. Almost any other player at the table can call your bet (or raise) and force you to play a flop against them out of position. It's a situation I like to exploit by smooth-calling early raisers when I'm in good position.

Maybe I'm still on tilt, but my 6-5 suited on the button looks good enough to call Phil "Unabomber" Laak's raise from under the gun. Unless the Unabomber has a pocket pair, he'll miss the flop completely—no pair, no draw—about two times out of three. Thanks to my superior position I should have a good shot at using sheer aggression to pick up this pot if he whiffs on the flop. My 6-5 may seem like a particularly weak hand to take to battle against a preflop raiser, but its weakness is what makes it such a good candidate: It's very unlikely to be dominated by whatever he is holding. I'd never call in this position with an easily dominated hand like A-7, K-J, or Q-J. There's too big a chance of getting myself into trouble, should I connect with the flop.

I call the $150 raise. Everyone behind me folds. There is $375 in the pot. Phil pulls his sweatshirt hood over his head, drops to the floor for three push-ups, and leaps to his feet with fists in the air. "Come on, Gordon, come on!" he taunts, throwing a few punches at an imaginary opponent. I have no idea where he gets that kind of energy. Neither does the amused dealer, it seems, who needs a few seconds to stop laughing before dealing the flop.

——THE FLOP——

Phil makes a show of counting the pot, $375, and then bets the same amount. He suddenly turns quiet, for which I am grateful. There is $750 in the pot, and it will cost me $375 to call.

Do I call, raise, or fold? What would you do?

First of all, I don't think Phil is bluffing here. The pot-size bet feels like an attempt to protect a strong but vulnerable hand. My best guess is that he's holding A-A, K-K, or A-Q and doesn't want to see another spade. Second, he quieted down during and after the bet. Talkative players who suddenly go quiet often have a hand that they want to play.

I, on the (literal) other hand, have a straight flush draw, and unless he's holding two big spades, I've got fifteen outs that will put me in front.* Using the Rule of Two, I know I have about a 30% chance of getting there on the turn, and, should I see the river,

---

* If he happens to be holding Q-Q, that would eliminate the Q♠ as one of my outs. But while this scenario is possible, it's statistically inconsequential, given the very small likelihood that (a) that's the hand he happens to have *and* (b) neither is a spade *and* (c) I happen to draw the last queen out of the deck.

I am better than 50% to make a straight or a flush. Given the 2-1 odds that I'm getting to call his bet, my Break Even Percentage to call and see the turn is 1 ÷ (2 + 1), or 33%.

I'm not getting *exactly* the right odds to call. I can make an argument that my implied odds later in the hand make it correct for me to call now, but there's no guarantee that Phil will continue betting should another spade appear on the turn. He reads me (and the rest of the world) very well. The bigger problem for me is that if I miss, I'm likely to face the very same decision on the turn . . . only with an even larger bet to call.

Then again, what am I doing thinking about calling? My first instinct should be to raise. Maybe his push-up/shadowboxing/taunting act kept me from running my mental script.

A straight flush draw is a hand to bring to war. While my chances of catching an out on the turn are only about 30%, the odds of me making a straight, flush, or straight flush by the showdown are better than 50%.

——THE BOARD——

My Opponent	My Hand	My Chances . . .
A-A or K-K	6♣5♣	56% (or 53% if he's holding the A♣ or K♣)
A-Q	6♣5♣	56% (or 53% if either card is a spade)
Q-Q	6♣5♣	42% (or about 41% if he has the Q♣)

In other words, unless he's holding Q-Q, I'm favored to win a showdown. And of the hands I've put him on, Q-Q is the least likely, as the queen on the board reduces the number of ways he could have two ladies from six ways to three. Besides, had he flopped top set, he probably wouldn't have made a bet that seemed designed to scare me off.

Poker rewards aggression. A raise here gives me two ways to win the hand: I can complete my draw or I can get Phil to fold. Add in my folding equity—the chance Phil will fold to my all-in raise—to the already better than 50% chance I have of drawing out, and this is a very profitable play. Think about it this way: If Phil were to go all-in and turn over A♠Q♥, would I call? Hell yes, I'd call!

In a tournament I'd have to be concerned about our

relative stack sizes. When survival is the goal, I'd rather avoid risking all of my chips in situations where I have only a small bit of positive equity. In a cash game, however, where I can replenish my stack with a short trip to the ATM, the positive equity decision is always the right decision. So why not risk all of my chips? Not only will I be making the most aggressive play I can—maximizing whatever fold equity I might have—but over the long haul it makes sense to exploit these situations to win as much money as I can.

I move all-in. Phil thinks for a minute or two before deciding to call. I show my 6-5 suited; he turns over A♥Q♥. "Come on, Gordon!" he shouts as he goes back into his shadowboxing routine. There is nearly $22,000 in the middle. My stomach starts to hurt a little bit.

The turn is the J♣. A blank, and no help to my hand.

"Survived the turn!" yells the Unabomber, playing to the crowd that has formed around the table. "I'm gonna felt you, Gordon!" He shifts from mock bravado to mock humility, as he pretends to root me on. "Come on, dealer, give my friend Phil Gordon a straight flush one time. Let's see a lucky deuce of spades on the river, one lucky deuce of spades!"

Here comes the river . . . but it's not a two. It's not a seven. It's not a spade. The Unabomber rakes a huge pot, much to the delight of the newly formed crowd, and I'm broke. Phil stands on his chair, unties his hood, and orders a round of shots for the table. With my money.

"Nice hand," I mumble. I'm not happy, but at least I have a plan: The next time I flop a set against Laak, I'm going to massively overbet the pot in exactly the same way I did with my straight flush draw. Instead of calling me with about a fifty-fifty chance to win, he'll be drawing to about a 2% chance to win. Hopefully, I won't have to wait too long.

❖ KEY ANALYSIS ❖

An all-in bet or raise in a situation where you are even a slight favorite is almost never "wrong" in a cash game, as it gives you two ways to win: showing down the best hand or convincing your opponent to fold.

FOUR IS THE MAGIC NUMBER

THE SITUATION: Three a.m., an eight-handed No Limit cash game at the MGM Grand, Las Vegas, after a night at the New York, New York, dueling pianos bar, my favorite "chill" hangout spot in town.

—NO LIMIT HOLD'EM—
Blinds $5/$10

POT: $35   **TO CALL:** $10   **POT ODDS:** 3.5–1

I'm in the cutoff seat and two players limped in from middle position. Raising here is a possibility. If I can knock out the dealer, I'll be playing from the best position throughout the hand even if I'm called, but with a small pocket pair maybe I'm better off seeing a cheap flop and hoping to connect with the board.

What would you do?

I call $10. The dealer folds, the small blind completes the bet, and the big blind checks.

——THE FLOP——

Presto! Fives are everywhere! Five players, five-oh in the pot, the four fives in my hand, and five double gin-and-tonics at the piano bar! It's going to be very hard for me to blow this one. All I have to do now is figure out how to maximize my returns.

Everyone checks to me. Do I bet, or check and hope the turn card improves somebody's hand? What would you do?

My strategy for playing when I flop quads is extraordinarily simple: Try not to smile, and slowplay, slowplay, slowplay. There's zero danger in giving someone a free card here, and I want action. The only way I'm likely to get any action is to give my opponents the chance to catch up. I check, and the dealer burns and turns.

——THE TURN——

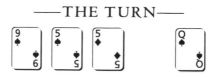

This is why we slowplay. Hopefully, the new flush and straight possibilities will help my opponents to overlook those two little fives in my hand.

The small blind checks, and the big blind bets $30. Seat 2 folds, but Seat 3 calls. The action is on me. There is $110 in the pot and it will cost me $30 to call.

Should I raise now or just call? What would you do?

It probably wouldn't be wrong for me to just call here, but I actually prefer to raise in this situation. If either player is on a draw, I want to get their money into the pot before the river closes out their chances of getting there. And if one of my opponents has the flush, I will probably get re-raised.

I raise to $75. The small blind folds; the big blind squirms but eventually calls. Seat 3 calls with even less conviction. There is $275 in the pot.

——THE RIVER——

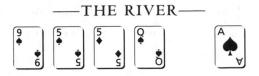

A very interesting card. Let's see how this plays out. . . .

The big blind immediately pushes all-in. Seat 3 tosses his cards into the muck.

What would you do?

If you don't know to call your opponent's all-in bet on the river when holding the absolute, immortal nuts, please return this book to the bookstore and take up canasta.

I call his bet and he turns over K♠Q♦ for the nut flush. It feels good to rake in a big pot, and it feels even better when Seat 3 tells everyone he had J-T. My raise on the turn earned me an extra $45!

—— ❖ K E Y   A N A L Y S I S ❖ ——

It's usually correct to slowplay when you flop an absolute monster, but rather than do mental jumping jacks, stay focused on how to extract the most money out of the pot.

THE POWER OF PERSUASION

THE SITUATION: A six-handed online No Limit Hold'em cash game. (Note: A version of this hand appeared previously on ESPN.com.)

——NO LIMIT HOLD'EM——
Blinds $5/$10

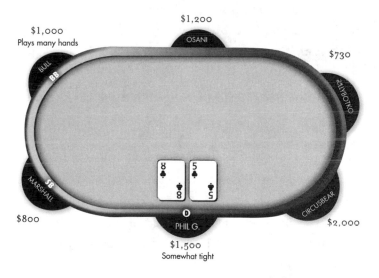

POT: $15   **TO CALL:** $10   **POT ODDS:** 1.5–1

I have been "running good" at this table, where I haven't shown down a losing hand in almost an hour and my opponents seem to respect my play. Everyone folds to me on the button. Both the small and big blind are tight, good players. What would you do? Limp, raise and try to steal the blinds, or fold?

Maybe my ego is getting the best of me, but I decide to raise. Steal the blinds with 8-5 suited? Why not? I hit the handy "Bet Pot" button, and the software calculates and announces that I've made it $35 to go.

The small blind does what he's supposed to—fold—but the big blind, a stubborn player, calls my raise. There is $75 in the pot.

——THE FLOP——

A good flop for me? Depends on if you're a "glass half-full" or a "glass half-empty" kind of thinker. The optimist in me sees that I've paired my eight, something that will happen on the flop only about once every three times I play two unpaired cards.

The half-empty part comes when the big blind leads out with a $35 bet. There is $110 in the pot, and it will cost me $35 to call.

What would you do?

One of the books that has had the greatest effect on my poker skills doesn't have anything to do with poker. In *Influence: The Psychology of Persuasion,* author Robert Cialdini explains the basic principles that allow one person to convince another to do what he or she wants him to do. What skill could be more valuable at the poker table? I try to use the book's techniques as often as I can, influencing my opponents to fold when they should raise and call, or bet when they should fold.

One of the most important principles, when trying to influence another person, is what Cialdini calls "Commitment and Consistency"—commit to a story and follow it through to the end. How does this apply to No Limit Hold'em? A while back I was talking to Howard Lederer about Phil Ivey's incredible run of success. Howard Lederer paid him the following compliment: "Phil can play any two cards like they are pocket aces. Once he plays a hand, his bets are completely consistent. They tell a believable story."

If I am going to continue with this hand, I have to come up with a compelling and consistent story. I was the preflop raiser, damn it, and I am going to take control of the betting. I know there is no way in the world that this guy slowplayed A-A, K-K, Q-Q, or J-J before the flop.

But I haven't done anything so far that would make him feel confident that I didn't have one of these hands.

Okay, what would I do if I did have A-A? The board isn't very scary—no flush draws, only a few straight draws. The fact that he didn't re-raise me before the flop tells me not only that he is unlikely to have any of the premium hands I mentioned in the last paragraph but that he probably doesn't have A-J either. With my imaginary aces I feel confident enough to raise about two thirds of the pot.

I raise his $35 bet $80 more, making it $115 to go.

I'll admit it: My confidence in my power to persuade takes a hit when the big blind calls the bet. Suddenly there's $305 in the pot.

He must have a hand like J-T, Q-J, J-9, T-9, or K-J, or maybe he's just being stubborn with A-8. He might also have been trying to make a move with a gutshot straight draw like Q-T, Q-9, or 9-7 and, despite my raise, decided that the odds made a call worthwhile. Nothing else makes much sense . . . unless, of course, he's slowplaying a set of deuces or eights. Good players will cede the initiative on hands like that and go for a big trap bet on the turn and river.

I hold my breath and pray to the poker gods for a five, or at least another eight. . . .

——THE TURN——

Not the card I was praying for, but it almost certainly wasn't the card he was looking for either. He checks to me.

What would you do?

Commitment and consistency. I can win this pot. With pocket aces or kings I'd likely bet half the pot, creating 3–1 odds for my opponent. He can call me with his draw, but he won't be getting the right odds.

I bet $150. The big blind calls quickly. The pot is up to $605.

The feeling in my stomach reminds me of the time I ate bad shellfish at an all-you-can-eat seafood buffet in Kansas City. "Are you aware, Mr. Gordon," says a little voice inside my head, "that you have just invested $300 with, pardon my French, a *turd* of a hand?"

Yes, I'm aware. Thank you for that, little voice.

——THE RIVER——

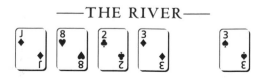

The actor inside me (yes, I have an actor inside me too, in case you missed my guest spots on *Less Than Perfect* and *Joey*)* announces that this is a very good card for my "pocket aces." There's simply no way that card could have helped him. All I have to do is bet.

I don't get a chance; the big blind leads out with a $200 bet. There is $805 in the pot, and it will cost me another $200 to call.

Can't say I expected that. Something, however, smells like rotten tuna. (Must. Stop. Thinking. About. Bad. Fish.)

♠ I raised preflop; he called out of position.
♠ I've been playing tight; he's a little loose.
♠ He bet the flop, I raised, he called.
♠ He checked the turn, I bet, he called.
♠ He led out with a $200 bet on the river, *underbetting* the pot.

Could he be bluffing a bluffer? Notice how he gave up control of the betting after my postflop bet and on the turn. Now he comes to life when there is no plausible way for that 3♠ to have helped his hand? This feels very much

---

* Unafraid to stretch my thespian talents to their limit, I played the role of the poker dealer on *Less Than Perfect*, and I played myself on *Joey*.

like a bluff. Then again, I've bluffed three times on this hand already.

What would you do?

Commitment and consistency. You're not going to scare me when I'm holding pocket aces! "How much would I raise if I had aces?" I ask myself for the third time.

"About $600," I reply to myself. (Note to self: Examine later the relationship between "acting" and odd internal dialogues.) "It'll look like you're *begging* him to call."

Erasing any nagging doubts from my brain—how does Phil Ivey live like this?—I summon whatever small amount of courage I have left and raise to $600.

The big blind hems and haws, or at least that's what I imagine he's doing on the other side of his Internet connection. It's stressful, but I remind myself that it's exactly what I want him to be doing. The more consideration he gives to the way I've played this hand, the more likely he'll be able to see that I *have* to be playing a big pocket pair. A strange sense of calm washes over me. I've already invested as much money as I'm going to, so nothing *worse* can happen to me. Either of the following will happen:

♦ My opponent will fold, I'll win the pot, and I'll become a little more Ivey-like, at least in my own mind.

♦ My opponent will call with a hand like Q-J and win the pot. I'll have lost some money, but I'll find a way, later in the session, to exploit his obvious lack of respect for my "monster" hands.

In truth, it doesn't matter how this hand ends. I committed to a course of action, and fired four bullets at the pot with exactly the sort of consistency that my bluff required.

If knowing what happened next really is important to you, then go to my Web site and you'll find the answer: www.philgordonpoker.com.

❖ KEY ANALYSIS ❖

Bluffs require commitment and consistency. Once you decide to represent a certain hand, be sure that all of your actions support the story you are hoping to sell. Be more willing to bluff against conservative thinking players. You can't bluff an opponent that isn't paying enough attention to your bets to "put you on the hand" that you're trying to represent.

CAN YOU SAY "OVERBET"?

THE SITUATION: A No Limit Hold'em cash game against good, though not professional, players.

——NO LIMIT HOLD'EM——
Blinds $25/$50

POT: $275   **TO CALL:** $175   **POT ODDS:** 1.6–1

It has long been poker's dirty little secret that there are players out there (1) who will raise any time they find the button in front of them, (2) who will fire two or three bluffs at a pot with absolutely nothing because "the flop got checked around," and (3) who will raise with any flush draw and will push all-in with any top pair. These guys, like the player in Seat 6, are known as overbettors.

I know all about overbettors: I used to be one. Those seeking proof need look no further than my heads-up performance at the 2003 Ultimate Poker Classic, where I attempted to dispatch "amateur" over-bettor Juha Helppi with a variety of substandard hands and overbets. *Warning: Due to the stunning violence used by Juha to eliminate me, the "professional," in what I'm guessing was record time, the video footage of the event is not recommended for small children or the faint of heart.*

My strategy for dealing with overbettors is now quite different from the one I employed against Juha. No longer will I try to counter blind aggression with even bolder, blinder aggression. My new strategy is much more effective:

♣ Wait patiently for profitable situations.
♣ Keep the pots as small as possible before the flop.
♣ Sacrifice a few small pots to the overbettor's relentless

barrage of bets and raises—even if there is a chance I have the best hand.

♣ Instill a false sense of confidence in my prey.

♣ Give him the rope he needs to hang himself when I have a great hand.

Back to the matter at hand . . . Mr. Overbettor, with $15,000 in front of him, raises to $200. I'm out of position, in the small blind with pocket fours. Do I re-raise, fold, or call?

What would you do?

My personal favorite hand to bring to battle against a habitual overbettor is a small pocket pair. I may wind up sacrificing some preflop equity when I call his raises from out of position (as I am about to do here), but when I flop a set (about 11% of the time), I am likely to get paid off in a very big way. No need to re-raise, as I want to keep the pot small before the flop—most of his biggest mistakes will happen after the flop.

I call the raise. There is $450 in the pot.

——THE FLOP——

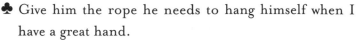

I've flopped my set. Bingo! Maximum extraction time. What would you do?

Normally, I'd bet out here and hope to get raised, but against a habitual overbettor, I think its better to just check. I'm not particularly worried about the two diamonds on the board—if he has a flush draw, he's going to overbet the pot on the flop, as the temptation to bet into "my weakness" will be too strong for him to resist.

I check and do my best to sit very, very still. The overbettor eyes me suspiciously. Does he sense a trap? Perhaps, but his animal instincts get the better of him. He pushes all-in, a massive, elephantine overbet of the pot. That is exactly what I was hoping for. I don't even need to ask you what you'd do, I hope.

I call, of course. He turns over A♦K♥.

The turn is the T♦, setting up a backdoor flush draw for the overbettor, which, I'll admit, makes me wonder if the poker gods have a vicious sense of humor.

As it happens, they do. The 3♦ appears on the river, giving him the runner-runner flush, and the overbettor smiles as he drags home all of my chips.

"Maybe next time, Gordon," he coos.

"Next time you want to risk all of your chips in a situation where I'm a 94.5% favorite to win, I'm happy to oblige," I reply, while trying (albeit unsuccessfully) not to sound bitter. As I'm walking to my safe-deposit box to reload, I take a deep breath and remind myself not to give lessons to the fish—unless they're reading my book!

❖ KEY ANALYSIS ❖

Against a habitual overbettor be willing to sacrifice a few small pots and occasionally take the worst of it before the flop so you can set yourself up to win a huge pot those times you flop a monster hand. Of course, setting yourself up to win a huge pot is no guarantee of winning said pot. . . . Poker can be a very cruel game.

IN THE BOARDROOM

THE SITUATION: Wall Street, where I'm playing a very big No Limit Hold'em cash game against a boardroom full of high-paid executives.

—NO LIMIT HOLD'EM—
Blinds $25/$50

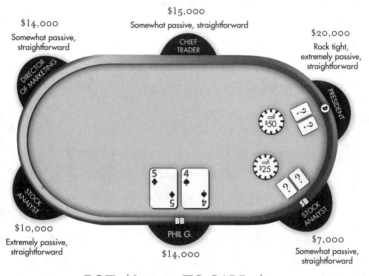

$14,000
Somewhat passive,
straightforward
DIRECTOR OF MARKETING

$15,000
Somewhat passive, straightforward
CHIEF TRADER

$20,000
Rock tight,
extremely passive,
straightforward
PRESIDENT

call $50

call $25

STOCK ANALYST

$10,000
Extremely passive,
straightforward

BB
PHIL G.
$14,000

STOCK ANALYST
SB

$7,000
Somewhat passive,
straightforward

POT: $150   **TO CALL:** $0

I have been invited to give a motivational speech to a roomful of stock traders at a big Wall Street financial services company. I love public speaking, and in reality, what traders do isn't so different from what poker players do: They try to invest their money in positive equity positions over many, many trials. There are many great poker players who were once stock analysts: *WPT* champion Alan Goehring, and Erik Seidel come to mind.

After my sixty-minute speech and some Q&A, I'm mingling at the bar and telling my favorite story: The time I saw Phil Hellmuth Jr. throw a chair after a bad beat. The company president, a guy whose yearly salary has seven digits (and whose net worth has nine), taps me on the shoulder. "Phil, we're thinking about putting together a little cash game in the boardroom. . . . You interested?"

It takes me about 0.7 seconds to decide, but I pause for a few seconds, hoping to hide my enthusiasm. "Um, sure, I guess that'd be okay."

Ninety minutes later I'm up $4,000. I love this game—the players are all very straightforward and very passive, giving my bets (and bluffs) more respect than they deserve. I've stolen four or five pots since we sat down and haven't been caught bluffing once. In fact, *no one* has been caught bluffing. This is the kind of game that an aggressive player (like yours truly) can just murder. I've won the last three pots with preflop raises without a confrontation. It seems like all I have to do is breathe on a pot to win it.

A new deal, and the president limps into the pot from the button. The small blind, a top stock analyst, completes the blind, and the action is on me with my powerhouse 5-4 offsuit. Given the tenor of the table, I could probably raise right now and take the pot.

What would you do?

I wouldn't mind raising, but after three in a row, I decide the more prudent action is to see the free flop. Although I don't think the prez is capable of a preflop slowplay, he's definitely capable of calling my raise in position. I check and see the flop.

——THE FLOP——

Pretty good flop for me, I'd say! The analyst checks to me from the small blind. I'm almost positive I have the best hand right now, but it's unlikely to get any better: I'll only make a full house by the river about 17% of the time. Do I check and hope to check-raise, or bet right out and hope someone has a hand they can call me with?

What would you do?

I think betting is right here. Unless the president has flopped a pair (or better), he's not going to bet if I check. These guys just don't make the nearly automatic continuation bets in position. They play a straightforward game of "betting when they have it and checking when they don't." Checking isn't likely to win me more money, not at this point, anyway.

I bet $100 and expect to win the pot. The president

88

calls somewhat tentatively; the small blind folds. There is $350 in the pot.

I'm not thrilled about getting called by the president, but I'm not ready to hit the panic button either:

♥ He probably would have raised before the flop with a pocket pair, and there's no way he'd play something like J-5 or J-4. I almost certainly have the best hand.
♥ My loose image could have convinced him to call me with hands that he might otherwise have thrown away.

My best guess is that he's got a jack. Considering that he didn't raise before the flop, the most likely possibilities are Q-J, J-T, or J-9. This is the good thing about playing against an opponent who plays a narrow range of hands and doesn't bluff very often—it's usually not too hard to put him on a hand.

——THE TURN——

That ten isn't such a bad card, unless he's holding J-T. Do I check or bet? What would you do?

I'm not slowing down—I don't want to give him a free card. If he has a pair of jacks, then a second ten on the river could "counterfeit" my two pair. If he has J-T, then I'll know it soon. A bet somewhere near half of the pot should close off most of his potential draws and give me a clearer picture of where I stand.

I bet $225. He thinks for about thirty seconds before raising to $700.

Gulp. At this point the pot has $1,275 in it, and I'm asked to call another $475. I'm getting about 3–1 odds to call.

What would you do?

I don't have to calculate any pot odds, engage in a long staredown, or do chip tricks while pretending to ponder a decision: This guy never bluffs. I put him on three or four potential hands after his postflop call, and only one of those hands would lead him to stick in a raise in this situation: J-T.

"Your jack-ten is good," I say as I throw my hand away. The president doesn't show me his hand, and I don't ask to see it. I know I was beat.

❧ KEY ANALYSIS ❧

When a player who never bluffs makes a bet or a raise, you have to put him on a big hand. Continuing on, even with a very good hand, is not smart poker.

FEELING ISOLATED

THE SITUATION: A nutty, shorthanded cash game at a friend's house. Richard has been using a big stack and hyperaggressive play to run over the table. I didn't bring enough cash with me to try to slow him down, and at this home game they don't take credit.

——NO LIMIT HOLD'EM CASH GAME——
Blinds $5/$10

$700   JILL

$400   QUINN

$1,400   SAVANNAH

$250   SCOTT   Somewhat tight

re-raise to $115

raise to $35

?? ?? RICHARD

$6,000   Plays many hands, kamikaze

A♠ A♥

BB   PHIL G.

$1,000

SB   DAWN $800

POT: $165   **TO CALL:** $105   **POT ODDS:** 1.6–1

Aggression is one of the keys to No Limit Hold'em, a fact that hasn't been lost on Richard in Seat 1. After buying in for $3,000 he has raised before nearly every flop. He has also wielded his big stack with just as much force after the flop, repeatedly compelling his opponents to make decisions for all of their chips. So far, it's working for him.

I've been waiting patiently for a chance to play back at him, and I've finally got it: I know that my pocket aces are a big favorite over whatever these two guys have. My goal is to convince my opponents to make the biggest mistakes possible.

What would you do?

My first instinct is, as usual, to raise. If I re-raise all-in, Scott is virtually pot committed with any two cards, and I'll be a huge favorite to win about $290: his $250 plus Richard's $35. The idea has its merits.

It suddenly occurs to me, however, that I've been presented with an interesting opportunity to trick Richard into using his aggressiveness against himself.

Suppose I just call Scott's re-raise. . . . It's going to seem like a weak play to Richard. When he looks over at Scott's stack, a measly $250, he might go for an isolation play, raising enough to put Scott all-in and

92

force me to fold my "weak" hand. Were I in his shoes, I'd consider that play for sure. Is this too fancy a play? Am I going to regret getting this tricky? It's a bit of a gamble, but I think the potential upside makes it worth the risk.

I call Scott's raise, and Richard goes into the tank. I can almost hear him thinking: Scott's on the short stack, Phil can't have much of a hand, and I raised preflop under the gun. Finally, just as I'm about to resort to prayer, Richard announces, "I'll put you both all-in."

Music to my ears. Scott grumbles a bit but shrugs his shoulder and calls. I don't waste any time grumbling or shoulder shrugging. I call quickly, flipping over my aces before Richard has a chance to expose his 7-7. Scott shows his hand, A-Q.

——THE FLOP——

I wince and wheeze and fight the urge to hide under the table, but the turn and river turn out to be innocuous. I take down a huge pot.

Against a superaggressive player be on the look-
out for opportunities to use that trait against
him. No move at the table is automatic: A careful examination of the situation in even "obvious" situations can often lead to more profitable
results.

EARLY TOURNAMENT PLAY

Cash game players play as if they're going to live forever. Tournament players know that the opposite is true—every tournament comes to an end. More times than not, it's a sudden and very painful end.

Good poker players tend to do better at tournaments than the bad ones, but short-term luck plays a huge role, often punishing the pros and rewarding the "schmoes." As a result most of the best tournament players have figured out ways to mitigate the effects of short-term luck.

Because tournaments use increasing blinds and antes to place an artificial constraint on the length of the event, the value of your chips changes over time. It's far less important to win small pots (or even big ones) early in a tournament than it is to capture the much larger pots created by big blinds and antes.

Because of this, I prefer to play very cautiously during the early stages of a tournament. I don't get involved in many hands. I'll pass up spots to "steal" the blinds (unless I happen to have a very strong hand) and rarely, if ever, bluff. I avoid "coin flips," or any situation where I have to risk all of my chips, unless I am a substantial favorite to win. My mantra is "low-risk, high-reward." Most of all, I pay very careful attention to the way my opponents are playing, looking for tells, bad habits, or other weaknesses that I'll be able to exploit later, when the stakes are higher.

SQUEAKY TIGHT

THE SITUATION: The tenth hand of a major tournament in Paris, France. Four hundred players remain.

POT: $75   **TO CALL**: $50   **POT ODDS**: 1.5–1

My eyes are already watering. Parisian poker clubs have yet to outlaw smoking. Earlier I paid $7 for a can of Coke at a restaurant along the Champs Élysées. This will likely be my last trip to Paris.

Focus, Phil. There's a tournament to win. Ten hands in and I've yet to play a pot. Everyone folds to me in the cutoff, where I find A–T offsuit. Do I limp in, raise, or fold?

What would you do?

In a cash game or the middle stages of a tournament (especially after the antes have kicked in), A–T offsuit in the cutoff represents a great opportunity to raise and steal the blinds. During the early stages of a tournament, however, there are three good reasons why larceny is the last thing on my mind:

- ♠ **There's not much to steal.** Both blinds combined make up less than one one-hundredth of my stack.
- ♠ **I'd rather not develop an image as a "blind stealer."** In fact, I want my opponents to think of me as the complete opposite (a "blind preserver"?), so they won't expect it when I do start stealing blinds.
- ♠ **I'd rather not develop an image as a pushover.** There is absolutely no way I am going to lose any significant amount of money playing A–T offsuit early in a tournament. If I did happen to play this hand, and someone re-raised me, I'd be gone before his bet hit the felt.

I want my fellow players to hold my obviously disciplined decision-making in high esteem. I want them to think of me as tight. *Squeaky* tight. When the stakes increase, my unblemished image will allow me to get away with murder.

For now the A-T goes straight into the discard pile.

❖ KEY ANALYSIS ❖

Maintaining a tight image early in a tournament—an image that can be exploited later for bigger payoffs—is much more important than winning a few early pots.

POISON IVEY

THE SITUATION: Day one of the 2004 *WSOP* championship. A Somalian minefield of players remain.

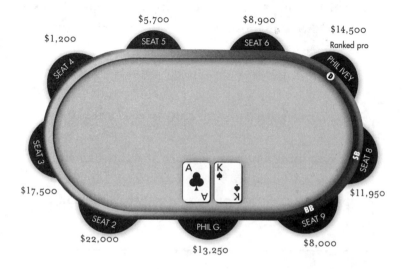

——NO LIMIT HOLD'EM TOURNAMENT——
Blinds $100/$200

$1,200

$5,700
SEAT 5

$8,900
SEAT 6

$14,500
Ranked pro
PHIL IVEY
D

SEAT 4

SEAT 3

SEAT 8
SB

$17,500

A♣ K♠

$11,950

SEAT 2

PHIL G.

BB
SEAT 9

$22,000

$13,250

$8,000

POT: $300   **TO CALL:** $200   **POT ODDS:** 1.5–1

Needless to say, with a field of more than twenty-five hundred players it is very unlucky to draw the great Phil Ivey. I can only hope my presence at the table gives Phil the same feeling. Somehow I doubt that's the case.

Bad draws aside, I'm dealt a "must play" hand from under the gun. My choices: raise or limp.

What would you do?

Well, you know me. I never limp in No Limit Hold'em, ever. This hand is worth playing, and it's worth playing for a raise. From early position I like to open with a raise of about two-and-a-half times the big blind. From under the gun my smaller raise will still get respect, and I'd rather not commit a truckload of chips to a hand that I'll likely have to play from out of position.

I raise to $500. Everyone folds except for Phil Ivey, who calls from the button. There is $1,300 in the pot. Ivey's call does not make me happy: He has more chips than I have, I'm out of position, and his last name is Ivey and mine is Gordon.

——THE FLOP——

I miss the flop completely, as I'm apt to do with A-K nearly two out of three times. Should I make a continuation bet here, or do I check and almost certainly face a bet from Ivey? What would you do?

This is an absolutely horrible flop for me. How many ways could Phil have connected with this board? Too many to count.

Lots of players overvalue A-K. Yes, it's a great hand before the flop. But with this flop my hand is worth just arginally more than toilet paper. While checking might seem like a wimpy play here, being a wimp is sometimes the smartest approach to the game. It's not just about aggression; it's about *selective* aggression.

I check. Ivey bets $600.

Does he have a better hand than I have? Is it time for an aggressive check-raise?

What would you do?

There is no way I'm going to put any chips in the pot here. I fold my hand. Phil Ivey graciously shows me his pocket fives, neglecting to utter the obligatory "Presto!"*

Yes, I might have won this pot had I led out with a scary enough bet. This hand is just one more illustration of the most critical factor at the table: position.

Moving on. With Ivey at the table, my tablemates and I are facing a very, very long day ahead of us.

✖ KEY ANALYSIS ✖

When deciding whether or not to make a continuation bet on the flop, let the texture of the board, your position, and the quality of your opponents guide you. There is a fine line between courage and foolishness.

---

* It's an old tradition from the RGP (rec.gambling.poker) newsgroup days: A player who wins with pocket fives declares "Presto!"

CHARITY CASE

THE SITUATION: Early stages of a charity tournament. About fifty inexperienced players remain.

—NO LIMIT HOLD'EM TOURNAMENT—
Blinds $25/$50

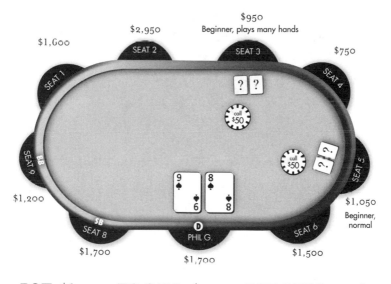

POT: $175   **TO CALL:** $50   **POT ODDS:** 3.5–1

I'm 9-8 suited with two limpers in front of me. Do I raise? First I check a few things. In position? Check.

Hand not likely to be dominated? Check. Plenty of chips? Check.

What would you do?

I'm not going to raise here, as inexperienced players just don't know enough to get out of the way—they just keep calling. I don't see anything wrong, however, with calling a couple of limpers with this hand.

The small blind and big blind both call, as I expected they would. There is $250 in the pot, with five players still contesting.

——THE FLOP——

In a limit game this would be an excellent flop for me—an open-ended straight draw without a flush in sight. In a No Limit game, however, expert opponents will usually make it prohibitively expensive to see the turn card.

The small blind bets $50. Clearly he's not an expert. Surprisingly, everyone folds to me. There is $300 in the pot, and it will cost me $50 to call.

What would you do?

When my opponent underbets the pot—as the small

blind has done here—chasing a premium draw is always profitable. With eight outs to a straight (any five or ten), I have a 16% chance of getting there on the turn. The pot odds create a Break Even Percentage of 1 ÷ (6 + 1), or 14%. This small bet from the small blind is a big gift.

Before taking action, however, I spend a few seconds wondering why he'd bet so little into this pot. I can think of four reasons:

1. He has a weak hand—maybe an ace with a low kicker—and is afraid of what's out there.
2. He has a strong hand—he could have flopped a set or made top two pair—and is trying to build a pot without scaring anybody off.
3. He's bluffing.
4. He has also flopped a straight draw and is semibluffing at the pot.

Given that three out of the four reasons I've listed put my opponent on a weak hand, it might seem tempting to fire back with a semibluff raise of my own.

What would you do?

The semibluff raise is one of the most abused and overused plays you will see at the poker table, especially in Low Limit Hold'em. I think raising is a huge mistake here. First,

I already have a positive equity play because of the small bet. Second, my opponent is so inexperienced that a raise will have nearly no chance to win the pot right away if he flopped a pair of aces—he's just not going to lay that top pair down.

Why would I pass up an opportunity to exploit a positive equity situation (calling a bet when the pot odds are in my favor) for a play that not only involves a bad financial decision (investing more money than my draw is worth) but leaves me exposed to a re-raise (eliminating my favorable odds and likely forcing me to fold my hand)?

I call the bet. There is $350 in the pot.

——THE TURN——

The small blind checks to me.

Thoughts of semibluffing once again creep into my mind. . . . After all, my opponent checked to me and showed weakness. His check presents a pretty good argument for betting, but there is also a case for checking behind him:

♦ The king was unlikely to have helped my hand. What, was I slowplaying A-K? Did I call two bets with K-7?

106

Neither will present a likely story to my opponent. My bluff at the pot is likely to look like just that, a bluff.

♦ I've got a free shot at making a nut hand. I can't tell you how many times I've bet in this spot, only to have my opponent come over the top of me with a check-raise. Or maybe worse: My opponent calls the bet, forcing me to bluff at the now-substantial pot with another bet on the river.

I think the smart play is to take the free card that's been offered to me. I check. There is still $350 in the pot.

——THE RIVER——

The small blind checks to me again.

This is an interesting spot. My pair of nines may be the best hand here. If it's not, a bet from me might get him to throw away a hand like a weak ace. Do I dare take a shot?

The truth is, I don't have a good read on my opponent. I've learned—the hard way—that when I have a medium-strength hand on the river against an opponent whose "story" I can't seem to piece together, I'm better off checking behind him.

I check. The small blind turns over A♥4♥ for a pair of aces and wins the pot.

Could I have bet enough to make him fold on the turn or river? Possibly, but it definitely would have seemed like a fishy bet, given the weakness that I'd shown throughout the hand. All told, I made positive equity decisions at every opportunity and enjoyed a very cheap look at a straight draw. Losing less than you could have is just as important as winning as much as you can.

❖ KEY ANALYSIS ❖

When an opponent underbets the pot and gives you the right odds to chase a draw, there's no need to get fancy with semibluff bets or raises. A simple "call" (and maybe a silent "thanks") should suffice.

GOING BROKE WITH ONE PAIR

THE SITUATION: Early in an online $200 buy-in multitable tournament at FullTiltPoker.com.

——NO LIMIT HOLD'EM TOURNAMENT——
Blinds $25/$50

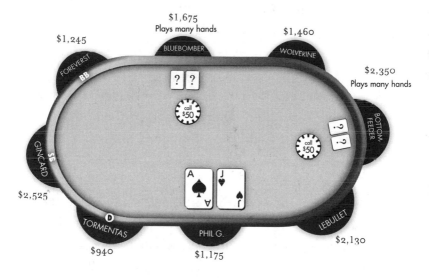

POT: $175   **TO CALL:** $50   **POT ODDS:** 3.5–1

Ace-jack suited isn't a powerhouse hand—it's easily dominated—but against two limpers who are playing a lot of hands, I really don't need a powerhouse hand to raise. I like to raise about the size of the pot in these situations, cutting down the odds for would-be callers and helping me limit the size of the competition.

I raise $125 and make it $175 to go. Everyone folds except for BottomFeeder, who calls my raise. There is $475 in the pot.

——THE FLOP——

A great flop for me, but BottomFeeder is first to act, and he bets $200. There is $675 in the pot. It will cost me $200 to call. Do I fold, call, or raise? What would you do?

What's with the $200 bet? BottomFeeder didn't show any aggression before the flop: He limped in, then called my raise, so he doesn't have a premium hand like A-A, K-K, or Q-Q. Would he have called with a hand like Q-J or J-T? Or a suited ace, maybe A-6 or A-4? Possibly. Maybe a middle pair, like pocket eights (or even worse for me, pocket sixes or fours)? A combination straight flush draw, like 8♦7♦? Is he just getting saucy with his chips, attacking a flop that was likely to have missed me?

The honest truth is that I don't have any idea where I stand on this hand, but I do know two things:

1. I have top pair with a great kicker.
2. There are a lot of turn cards that I don't want to see.

I think I have to raise here. I raise his $200 by $400, making the bet $600 to go. BottomFeeder calls. There is $1,675 in the pot.

——THE TURN——

BottomFeeder checks to me.

I've really put myself in a fix here. My bet on the flop wasn't a good number. Now I am pretty much committed to the pot, but I can't bet enough to chase out a potential flush draw. I probably should have moved all-in after the flop. But there aren't any mulligans in poker. . . . It's time to make a decision. With just $400 left, what would you do?

My best option here, I think, is to push all-in and hope that my hand is the best. I can't put a lot of pressure on him, but moving all-in seems reasonable and consistent. Given the size of the pot, I fully expect him to call, and I can only hope he has the worst hand and misses on the river.

I bet my last $400.

Before I go further with this hand, remember the situation. This is the early part of a tournament where I want to play tight, avoid marginal situations, and slowly build my stack while getting a read on my opponents. So why the heck am I going all-in with one pair when I neither know much about my opponent nor have a good read on his hand?

Good questions to ponder, as BottomFeeder quickly calls. I show my pair of jacks, but he shows 4♣4♥ for a set. He has played this hand very, very well. Not only am I drawing totally dead, but I've broken one of my cardinal rules: Don't go broke with one pair. Even worse, I've broken this rule during the early stage of a tournament. I feel like a big, smelly, rotten piece of tuna hanging from a bloody treble hook.

❖ KEY ANALYSIS ❖

Don't go broke with one pair. My primary mistake here was to invest so much money in top pair on the flop that I built a pot I couldn't afford to get away from.

STEPPING UP TO THE MIKE

THE SITUATION: Early in a free-roll tournament at the Venetian. Winner gets a Lotus sports car. About three hundred players remain. (A version of this hand originally appeared in my weekly column on ESPN.com's poker page.)

——NO LIMIT HOLD'EM TOURNAMENT——
Blinds $25/$50

POT: $225   TO CALL: $150   POT ODDS: 1.5–1

We're at the Venetian's brand-spanking-new poker room, one of the prettiest in the world, where the best of the best are gathered for a celebratory opening night tournament. Brunson, Reese, Greenstein, Harman, and Ivey are all there. The winner drives home in a new Lotus, though I'm 100% certain that there is no chance in hell my 6'9" frame will fit into a car that looks like it was built for someone a foot shorter. Maybe I can take out the back seat.

Mike Matusow, perhaps hopped up on free Coronas, has been on a kamikaze mission. Granted, it's a freeroll, and the rapidly increasing blind structure (doubling every twenty minutes) calls for faster-than-normal play. But Mike seems intent on flaming out, seemingly playing and raising every hand.

I stay out of the way for the first eighteen minutes or so. Mike has, so far, managed to avoid self-annihilation, adding nearly $2,000 to his stack with pure, uncontrolled aggression.

When Mike raises three times the big blind from middle position and everyone folds to me in the cutoff seat, my A-T is a decent hand, especially against a guy who's playing like any two will do. But do I have enough to call a raise? Do I re-raise?

What would you do?

Against loose players, re-raising their opening raises is often an excellent strategy. In this particular case, I have a long list of good reasons to do so:

♣ A solid re-raise—say $450 to go—should intimidate the players left to act behind me, forcing them to fold anything but a truly premium hand.

♣ I very well could have the best hand.

♣ I've been playing very tight, and Mike, regardless of whether he'd admit it in public, respects my play. He's very unlikely to call my re-raise out of position with a hand like A-J or K-Q. If he calls, I'll have a very good idea what kind of hand he's on.

♣ If he re-raises, he's almost definitely going to go all-in. I'll have a tough decision to make, but I can still lay down the hand and have $2,450 remaining—plenty of chips to stay competitive.

♣ I'll take control of the betting. If Mike misses the flop—something that will happen more times than not—my post-flop continuation bet should be enough to win.

I re-raise to $450.

Everyone folds to Mike, who takes an uncharacteristically quiet minute to consider his options. He eventually decides to call my raise. There is $975 in the pot.

My brain kicks into high gear, engaging in a little multi-level thinking, before the dealer has a chance to burn the top card:

Level One. What do I have? A-T is a pretty good hand, but Mike's quick call has me concerned that it's not the *best* hand.

Level Two. What does Mike have? My best guess is a small to medium pocket pair. He could also have a suited ace or connector. I don't think he has A-K or A-Q—he would have re-raised me with either of those hands—but he might have A-J.

Level Three. What does Mike think I have? This is the first hand I've gotten involved in. He respects my play and knows that I like to play tight poker in the early rounds of a tournament. He has to put me on A-Q or better.

——THE FLOP——

Mike checks to me. What would you do?

Not only do I think I have to bet here, but I think I have to move all-in.

- ♥ I probably don't have the best hand right now. I want him to fold.
- ♥ An all-in bet doesn't feel "fishy." It's certainly consistent with my holding A-K or A-Q, and I might even make the same play with A-A, K-K, or Q-Q.

116

♥ If Mike has a small pocket pair, it will be nearly impossible for him to call. Even if he does, I still have ten outs and will win the hand about 40% of the time.

♥ My bet should be enough to get him to fold A-J or Q-J.

♥ Regardless of what he might call with, I have outs—any jack will make a straight.

♥ Several very beautiful celebrities have already busted out and headed for the nightclub Tao. If Mike busts me here, well, I know where I'll go to console myself.

I move all-in. Mike thinks for about fifteen seconds before flipping his pocket sevens faceup into the muck. "Too bad it didn't come K-Q-7," he mutters.

Yep. Too bad. As I rake in the pot, I see Shannon Elizabeth (Nadia from *American Pie*) heading off to join the rest of the crowd at Tao. I might just start playing like a kamikaze myself.

❖ KEY ANALYSIS ❖

Isolating a loose preflop player with a re-raise can be very profitable. After you take control of the betting, back it up with an aggressive bet postflop.

LOST AT SEA

THE SITUATION: The first round of a $100 buy-in tournament aboard a cruise ship. Seventy-five players remain.

——NO LIMIT HOLD'EM TOURNAMENT——
Blinds $25/$50

POT: $325   **TO CALL:** $25   **POT ODDS:** 13–1

I'm on a cruise. A Caribbean cruise. In all honesty, I'm not all that thrilled about it. It seems I've booked a vacation for a friend and me on the geriatric *Titanic*. The over/under on the number of passengers who die of old age (or boredom) before the boat hits Jamaica, according to a local oddsmaker (my friend), has been set at three.

I've just finished losing $5 and a mai tai to a septuagenarian shuffleboard shark when I hear a glorious announcement over the loudspeaker: "Attention passengers . . . please join the captain in the gaming lounge at three p.m. for a $100 buy-in No Limit Texas Hold'em tournament." Maybe this cruise won't be so bad after all.

It's the very first hand and I'm dealt A-7 suited in the small blind. Five players, including the captain, limp into the pot in front of me.

What would you do?

Well, clearly, this is a "no fold'em hold'em" convention. I could, perhaps, raise and hope to take the pot right away, but I'm seriously afraid that these people won't know enough to fold. The sobering prospect of heading back to the shuffleboard pit lends me restraint. I complete the small blind, and the big blind checks as well. Seven players see the flop, just like the Tiltboy home game.

──THE FLOP──

The good news: I've flopped top pair. The bad: I'm out of position with six players behind me and I have no clue if I have the best hand. I can check and see what develops, or I can bet right out.

What would you do?

Hey, I got a free look at the flop, but that doesn't mean I have to go crazy here. I decide to check and see what develops. I'm not looking for tells—especially the shaky hands tell, since everyone at the table, with the possible exception of the captain, has shaky hands.

"Merv," or so says his name tag, is seated on my left and bets $50. Yes, he bets $50 into the $350 pot. I'm still shaking my head in disbelief when all five players remaining call in front of me.

What would you do?

I make a crying call, that's what I do. I hate my hand, but I just can't bring myself to fold when I'm getting 12—1 on my money and have top pair.

—THE TURN—

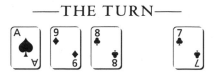

I made two pair on the turn. Is it good? I still have no clue. Other than scratching your head, what would you do?

Despite my hand's improving, I'm not even going to think about betting out here. I could have the best hand or I could be completely dominated. There are just too many straight possibilities. Remember, I'm up against six players! Maybe I *should* have raised before the flop.

I check again. Merv, unperturbed, squints, adjusts his reading glasses, and then bets all his chips in one motion. Everyone sneers at Merv, including me. One by one they fold, and it is up to me.

What would you do?

What you should do is be more careful about the cruise line you book your vacation on. I really don't have any idea what is going on, and I don't think any of them do either. The very worst case: I head back to the poolside shuffleboard pit. I call.

Merv takes the hand ranking chart out of his front pleated pocket and scans up and down. "What do you call this? I think it's called a straight," he says with a smirk as he turns over J-T and the nuts. It's going to take a lucky full house to beat him, but the dealer burns and turns a blank and I'm the first player eliminated.

"Ever since I saw you do that hand ranking card thing to Phil Hellmuth in Aruba on the first season of the *WPT*, I've been waiting for an opportunity to do that to a pro," Merv says with a smile. "I'm a big fan. Will you sign my name tag before you go?" The other players at the table look startled, like deer in headlights. Maybe it's just BOTOX. I get up from the table, shake his hand, sign his name tag, and seriously consider jumping overboard.

❖ KEY ANALYSIS ❖

Just because you get to see the flop doesn't mean you have to lose your entire stack if you flop a pair. In "no fold'em hold'em" affairs, hands like top pair, or even two pair, rarely turn out to be the winner.

FLUSHED

THE SITUATION: Early in an online tournament at FullTiltPoker.com. Nearly two hundred players remain. The average stack is about $2,200.

—NO LIMIT HOLD'EM TOURNAMENT—
Blinds $20/$40

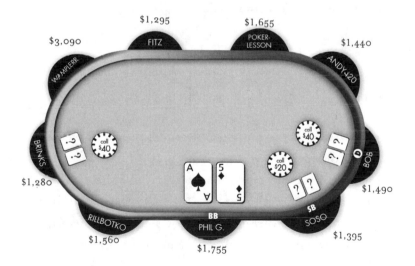

POT: $160   **TO CALL:** $0

Against supertight players this might be a spot to raise and try to steal the pot. I have a tight image, no one has showed strength, and I might have the best hand. Do I try to raise the limpers, or do I check and see a flop?

What would you do?

In the early stages of a tournament—especially an online tournament—gamblers never seem to be in short supply. I don't want to start mixing it up now, with a hand that's easily dominated, for a relatively small pot. I'll rap the table and see a flop. There is $160 in the pot.

——THE FLOP——

I flopped the nut flush draw. SoSo checks to me.

I obviously have a great draw in this situation, but in No Limit Hold'em—where players have the maximum amount of control over the size of the pot—drawing hands are very overrated. I've got a tough choice here: Check and see what develops, or make a bet and hope to win the pot right away.

What would you do?

Against three opponents, I decide to check and see what happens. . . . Brinks bets $40 and gets called by Bob on the button. SoSo folds. There is $240 in the pot, and it will cost me $40 to call. I could raise and try to take the pot, or I can call the $40 and see the turn.

What would you do?

My first thought is always to play aggressively. That $40 bet looks pretty weak. I can raise in the hopes of winning the pot right now: Even if I get called, I'll have plenty of outs. Still, I'm not entirely sure a raise is the correct play. Maybe its time for a quick appeal to the Rule of Two. With nine spades left in the deck, I have about an 18% chance of catching one on the turn. My Break Even Percentage is $1 \div (6 + 1)$, or 14.2%.

As it turns out, these guys are giving me the right odds to chase my flush. I'm actually getting the best of this situation by calling. Instead of exerting pressure here—and potentially putting myself in harm's way—I'll try to preserve my chips, keep the pot small, and see what happens on the turn.

I call the $40 bet, bringing the pot to a total of $280.

——THE TURN——

That's a card I'm happy to see. I've got the nut flush! Do I bet out, or get sneaky with a slowplay?

What would you do?

When I improve my hand on the turn, especially after playing passively on the flop (as I did when I checked and called), I'll usually switch to a more aggressive tack. Since I have the nut flush, the only hands I have to fear from my opponents are sets or two pair that might become full houses on the river. They are, at best, drawing to ten outs, a likelihood of about 20%. If I bet half the pot here, a potential caller will only be getting 3–1 odds to call. For calling to be correct he's going to have to have a hand that beats me at least 25% of the time. There is no hand that will beat me 25% of the time, so calling my bet will definitely be a mistake. Added bonus: The bet is small enough that an opponent might call with a flush draw.

I bet $140. Both Brinks and Bob decide to call. There is $700 in the pot.

Whoops. I didn't account for the possibility that *both* players would call! The extra money in the pot actually makes calling with a hand like two pair a good money decision. Please don't pair the board. Please don't pair the board. Please don't . . .

——THE RIVER——

K♠ 7♣ 2♣ 8♣   7♣

. . . pair the board. Argh! I no longer have the nuts—
a full house will beat me—but I still have the nut flush. Do
I lead with another bet, or check and see what happens?

What would you do?

I may be playing like a wimp, but after careful consideration I decide to check. If both of my opponents
check behind me, I'll want to kill myself. My fantasy
scenario is for one of them to do the betting for me . . .
with a weaker hand than mine.

I check. Brinks bets $240. Bob folds. There is
$940 in the pot, and it will cost me $240 to call. I'm
getting nearly 4–1 on my money.

Poker is an evil game, isn't it? My gut tells me that
I'm looking down the barrel at a full house, but the tiny
bet makes it impossible (or at least a huge mistake) to
fold. I only have to have the best hand about 20% of the
time to make calling the correct play.

I call. He turns over (of course) 8♥7♥, the dreaded
full house.

"nh," I type as I briefly consider throwing my lap-
top into the pool. The only good news is that I'm still

in the tournament. Many other players would have gone broke with this hand.

❖ KEY ANALYSIS ❖

I probably got too fancy on the turn against two opponents—a bigger bet would have earned me the pot, or at least made it a bigger mistake for them to call. I certainly would have bet more had I known both of my opponents were going to call. When there is a possibility of a multiway pot, increase the amount you're willing to bet after the flop and turn.

SOMETIMES YOU'RE JUST GOING TO GO BROKE

THE SITUATION: The first day of the *WPT* Commerce Tournament. Around five hundred players remain. The average stack is about $12,000.

—NO LIMIT HOLD'EM TOURNAMENT—
Blinds $100/$200

POT: $900   **TO CALL:** $600   **POT ODDS:** 1.5–1

A lot of players—including many great ones, like Gus Hansen, Daniel Negreanu, Mike Matusow, and Dave "the Devilfish" Ulliott—like to play the role of the "table captain" during the early stages of a tournament. They play a lot of hands and bully their opponents in the hopes of building a big stack early. When successful, they use that big stack to keep playing a lot of hands and bullying their opponents later. They go broke early in some tournaments, but there is always a cash game (and usually a very big one) waiting for them.

While it works for some, I don't usually like to be the table captain during the early part of a tournament—I'd rather create a tight image that I can exploit later when the stakes are actually meaningful. I'll generally stay out of the way of a table captain . . . unless I pick up a big hand and a chance to win a big pot.

Seat 4 (this table's self-anointed captain) has been raising with a lot of hands, two or three per round. I sense she's a good player—not completely reckless, especially after the flop. Most of the players at the table share my philosophy of playing tight early, and she's taking advantage of that fact in a masterful way. I've managed to avoid playing a hand against her so far.

That's about to change. Ace-king is a premium hand. I'm definitely going to play it. So, the big question is, do I re-raise or just call?

What would you do?

I go through my mental checklist:

♠ I'm in position, so smooth-calling is definitely a possibility. I'd almost never just smooth-call if I were out of position. I'd try to win the pot before the flop.

♠ How good is my opponent after the flop? Pretty good, which is a reason to re-raise. I'm probably better off taking the pot without a flop.

♠ How strong is her hand? She's probably not raising with complete junk, because she's in middle position. Any pocket pair, any ace down to eight or nine, and K-Q are possible and likely. This is another reason to re-raise—to get more information about the strength of her hand. (Not to mention getting more money into the pot while I probably have the best hand.)

♠ Will she call my re-raise with a worse hand than mine? Probably, which is a good reason to re-raise. If she'd fold a hand like A-Q or A-J to my re-raise, I might consider just smooth-calling and praying for an ace on the flop.

♠ How strong is my hand? Well, I need an ace or a king on the flop if I want to feel at all comfortable, and that's only going to happen about 35% of the time. Here's another vote for the re-raise.

♠ How many chips do I have? An average stack. There are plenty of chips in play right now in relation to the size of the blinds, so this is not much of an issue.

After due consideration and adding the fact that I've been playing very tight, I select my play: a re-raise. I up the bet to $2,000.

Everyone folds to the captain, who ponders her move and finally decides to call. There is $4,300 in the pot.

——THE FLOP——

I felt a moment of dread when she called my pre-flop raise, but that's all gone now. . . . I hit the jackpot with this flop! I don't think there's any chance that this player has slowplayed A-A, K-K, or Q-Q out of position against me. I'm very much hoping she has A-Q, A-J, or A-T, hands that are consistent with her preflop actions and will provide plenty of excitement given this flop. There aren't really any other hands that matter. If she has called me with a medium pocket pair, I'll only have to breathe on the pot to win it.

She checks to me. Should I check (slowplay) or bet? What would you do?

I can't imagine that she has a draw good enough to call a bet, but I might be able to get her to call something small, say, a third or half the pot, with A-J or A-T. In doing so I also prevent her from taking a free shot at drawing to trips or a gut-shot straight.

I bet $1,500. "Raise," she announces almost immediately. "Make it $5,000."

Can't say I expected that one. Think, Phil. What could she have? As I said, she would have re-raised me before the flop with A-A, K-K, or Q-Q, so a set seems unlikely. She's also the type of player (that is, a good one) who would lead out with a bet had she flopped a set, hoping to get raised. I don't think she's got a set. She must put me on a very good hand as well, or she thinks I missed the flop completely and have a small pocket pair.

Could she have a straight? No way she called my preflop re-raise with J-T, even if it was suited. I'm not worried about that hand at all.

Her raise is big, but not so big that she can't get away from this pot should I come over the top all-in. She could be hyperaggressively playing A-J or A-T. If she thinks I'd re-raise before the flop and then make a continuation bet with a medium pocket pair, she could even be bluffing or semibluffing.

Does she have a huge hand or just a huge amount of courage? My options seem clear: Call, fold, or go all-in.

What would you do?

I decide that the pot is big enough and that there

is a high enough likelihood that I have the best hand. I want to take it down now. Maybe I'm just putting my opponent on a hand I can beat, but in the little fantasy I've carved out, she has A-Q, will call my all-in bet, and will be completely dominated.

I re-raise all-in. She calls in a flash. "You flop a set?" she asks. Music to my ears—she *must* have A-Q or A-K.

"Nope, just top two," I say, and flip over my cards, sure that I've got a winner.

"Huh," she sighs, slow-rolling a J-T—the heart-piercing nut straight. "I thought you were better than that."

I so badly want to say something like, "At least I'm good enough not to call 14% of my chips out of position with J-T offsuit before the flop," but I restrain myself. I leave that sort of banter to the other Phils.

I collect myself and stare at the board while the dealer burns and turns, but the turn card is a blank. My buddy, Antonio Esfandiari, comes over and comforts me with a hand on my shoulder. The dealer burns and shows the river card. My hand does not improve, and, despite Antonio's efforts, my attitude doesn't either.

"Still learning the game, I guess," I reply as I collect my iPod, my backpack, and what little dignity I have remaining and head for the exit. I see one of my favorite fish swimming out of the tournament room at the same time, announcing that he's just busted out and is heading for a high-stakes cash game.

I'm suddenly feeling a lot better.

❖ KEY ANALYSIS ❖

Sometimes you just go broke. You'll catch a hand so strong, a hand so unlikely to be beaten, that you ignore any evidence that suggests the contrary. There's nothing you can do but take the beat with poise and professionalism.

TIME FOR BED

THE SITUATION: Last hand before the end of the first day of the 2004 *WSOP* championship event. Thousands of players remain.

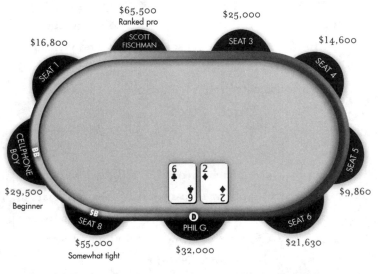

——NO LIMIT HOLD'EM TOURNAMENT——
Blinds $300/$600 with $75 antes

$65,500
Ranked pro
SCOTT FISCHMAN

$25,000
SEAT 3

$16,800
SEAT 1

$14,600
SEAT 4

CELLPHONE BOY
BB
$29,500
Beginner

SEAT 5

$9,860

SB
SEAT 8
$55,000
Somewhat tight

D
PHIL G.
$32,000

SEAT 6
$21,630

POT: $1,575   **TO CALL**: $600   **POT ODDS**: 2.6–1

Cell Phone Boy, seated in the big blind, gets a phone call during the deal of the last hand of the day: "Yeah, I'm still in it. . . . It's crazy, man. . . . I'm, like, sitting at the table with Scott Fischman and that guy from *Celebrity Poker Showdown*, Phil Something-or-other. . . ."

I'm sitting comfortably with just over fifty big blinds. I have far surpassed my "goal" for the day, and I feel great about the way I've played. There is absolutely no reason to get involved with a junk hand here, right?

What would you do?

I love playing the last hand of the day from nearly any position, and this hand is no exception. In tournaments that are spread across multiple days, the end of the first or second day is a lot like the bubble you'll face later in the tournament. Unless a player is severely short stacked and feeling reckless, he's not going to want to get busted out on the last hand of the day. My decision here gets an added boost from the fact that the two players left to act—a tight small blind and Cell Phone Boy, who's clearly accomplished his own more modest goal of surviving day one—seem even less likely to want to mix it up.

I raise to $2,400, four times the size of the big blind. The small blind folds, but in a surprise move Cell Phone Boy calls. There is $5,775 in the pot.

——THE FLOP——

Believe it or not, this is actually a very good flop for me. If he had a strong ace, he probably would have re-raised me. He's most likely playing a pocket pair. As long as it isn't 7-7 or 3-3, I should be able to get him to fold if I make a decent bet or raise.

Cell Phone Boy checks to me. Do I check or bet?

What would you do?

I want to bet the same amount I would bet if I were holding a big ace in my hand. A little more than half the pot should do it. I bet $4,000.

He shuffles his cards for a minute, shows pocket jacks, and tosses them into the muck. "I hate that crap," he says as he rises from his seat, already dialing a number on his cell phone.

❧ KEY ANALYSIS ❧

The end of a day in a multiday tournament is a lot like the bubble—players don't want to go broke on the last hand. With aggressive play you can often exploit their haste to get away from the table.

MIDDLE TOURNAMENT PLAY

Once I reach the middle stages of a tournament—generally around the time when the antes kick in—my squeaky-tight strategy gets flipped on its head.

In the middle of the tournament there is a lot more money at stake before the flop. This makes it far more worthwhile to use preflop raises and good position to steal pots, regardless of the strength of my hand, without a confrontation. Hopefully, my opponents have observed how tight I've been playing during the early stages and will give my raises a little more respect than they deserve. At the same time I'll get to use the mental profiles I've had time to develop for each opponent, attacking the players who are susceptible to aggression, and looking for spots to trap the ones who aren't.

There is another major shift that tends to emerge in the middle rounds—stack size becomes a factor, greatly affecting the way I decide to play. If I'm lucky enough to be sitting behind a big stack, this is the time when I will start using it, putting pressure on my opponents with aggressive preflop raises. I'm forced to take a somewhat different tack when I'm on the short stack. While it doesn't make too much sense to push all-in before the flop when I have plenty of chips to cover the blinds and antes, I won't hesitate to do so when my chips start to dwindle. I'd much rather be overaggressive with a short stack (while my all-in raises are still scary enough to get my opponents to fold or, if they don't, while doubling up is still meaningful) than to let my chips get blinded off without a fight.

IMAGE ISN'T EVERYTHING, BUT IT'S CLOSE

THE SITUATION: A very small buy-in multitable tournament at the Palms Casino, Las Vegas. About one hundred players remain. The blinds have just increased to $100/$200, and $25 antes are being collected for the first time.

—NO LIMIT HOLD'EM TOURNAMENT—
Blinds $100/$200 with $25 antes

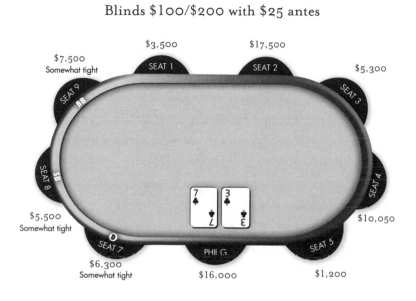

POT: $525   **TO CALL:** $200   **POT ODDS:** 2.6 1

Throughout the early stages of this tournament I've been playing very, very tight. I have yet to show down a loser, and the hands I've exposed have been quality: pocket aces, A-K suited, and wired jacks.

When everyone folds to me, I consider my options: raise or fold. Limping in is not an option I consider after the antes start—it is strictly raise or fold.

What would you do?

Remember that tight image I was going to exploit later on? "Later on" usually begins around the time the antes kick in. Yes, 7-3 is an awful hand, but I have plenty of chips and I'm in the cutoff—great position for stealing blinds—with three average stacks behind me. The two players in the blinds seem to be playing very tight poker, creating a perfect spot to stick in a good-size raise—about three-and-a-half times the big blind should do—and hope I can take down an easy pot.

I raise to $700. Everyone folds except the small blind, who calls. There is $1,825 in the pot.

Whoops . . . that wasn't supposed to happen. I'm not at all happy about his call.

——THE FLOP——

That's a fairly disconnected flop. The small blind checks to me, showing weakness. Do I make a continuation bet and try to steal the pot, or should I just check and give up? What would you do?

In a situation like this a continuation bet is almost mandatory. I represented strength before the flop, and there's no reason to stop now. I sense the weakness, and

I'm ready to pounce. About half the pot sounds right to me.

I bet $1,100 into the pot. The small blind seems to consider my bet for a minute, then calls. There is $4,125 in the pot.

——THE TURN——

There aren't any good cards for me in the deck, so I'm not disappointed to see the ace on the turn. The small blind checks to me again.

A big part of me thinks that I am in huge trouble. I have built a $4,000-plus pot against a solid player and I have virtually no chance of winning a showdown.

Let's cycle through some of the hands he might have called me with on the flop. Pocket queens, or any big overpair, seems pretty unlikely, given that he didn't re-raise me before the flop. He's played tight so far and, more important, has seen *me* play tight so far, so he probably wouldn't have called my preflop raise with a hand like A-9 or A-4.

Does he have a very big hand, like A-Q or 9-9? Probably not, given that he's played passively throughout the hand. With two flush cards on the board it's hard to imagine that he wouldn't have put in a bet somewhere along the line to try to protect his hand.

Is he on the flush draw? Maybe, but he might have bet the flop with just a flush draw.

That leaves two real possibilities:

1. He has a hand like K-Q or Q-J and is afraid I have something better.
2. He has a medium pocket pair, like tens or eights, he's put me on a hand like A-K, and he thinks I missed the flop.

In either case the A♠ on the turn is a great card for me. Since the size of the pot ($4,125) is rapidly approaching the size of his remaining stack ($6,700), any pot-size bet will commit him to risking all of his chips on this hand. My options are clear: Fire the third bullet and make a big bet, or check and give up. What would you do?

Given his tentative play and my squeaky-tight image, I really don't think he will call my bet. I bet $4,000. Small blind shakes his head in disgust and throws his hand into the muck. I definitely *do not* show him my cards—I want to maintain that tight image I've worked so hard to obtain.

"Good laydown," I say, as I take one last peek at my 7-3 and toss it away.

I effectively used my table image, my position, my knowledge of my opponent, and my courage to win that pot. Stealing and bluffing from late position are critical to winning tournaments. If I can pull off just a few successful steals like this one in the middle stage of this tournament, I'll be well on my way to the final table.

❖ KEY ANALYSIS ❖

Good poker players change gears, loosening or tightening their play as the situation demands it.

THE SPEECH

THE SITUATION: A $5,000 buy-in No Limit Hold'em tournament. Around two hundred players remain. The table is being televised for a later broadcast.

──NO LIMIT HOLD'EM TOURNAMENT──
Blinds $500/$1,000 with $100 antes

POT: $2,400   **TO CALL:** $1,000   **POT ODDS:** 2.4–1

Ace-jack, a hand that can cause you all kinds of problems, gets overrated by a lot of inexperienced players. That said, I'm down to thirty-nine big blinds, a little below the average stack. When everyone folds to me in late-middle position, do I fold the A-J, limp in and try to see a cheap flop, or raise?

What would you do?

Limping is not an option for me. . . . Limping

146

is not an option for me. . . . Limping is not an option for me. When I'm first to the pot, I *always* raise, no exceptions. There are many other great players who disagree with me—Daniel Negreanu, Gus Hansen, Erick Lindgren, and Antonio Esfandiari, just to name a few— but this is the style I play. If I'm going to be the first to commit chips to the pot, I am going to raise or fold. End of story.

So do I raise here? There is a decent case to be made for folding . . . both the button and Howard Lederer are short stacked. If either of them move all-in against me, I'll have a very tough decision, and I'll probably be forced to call them with a hand that might be dominated.

A meteor could also hit the card room. I can't be afraid of everything. Raising is clear. From middle position I like to raise between three and three-and-a-half times the size of the big blind. Given that the big blind (let's call him the Loose Guy) has been playing a lot of hands, I'll opt for the higher end of the spectrum in the hopes of scaring him away.

I make it $3,500 to go. The Loose Guy calls—so much for discouraging him. There is $8,400 in the pot.

——THE FLOP——

Loose Guy checks to me. Do I check (and hope to trap him on the turn) or do I bet?

What would you do?

Unless he's slowplaying A-K or A-Q, I'm likely to have the best hand here. A-K is very unlikely, I think. He probably would have re-raised with that hand. Since I have little chance of improving my hand on the turn or the river, there's a flush draw on the board, and there are some straight possibilities, I would not be disappointed to win this pot right now.

A $6,000 bet seems about right to me, leaving me with $30,000, a nice, round number. I toss my bet into the middle. Loose Guy seems to consider for a moment before calling. There is $20,400 in the pot, and a growing uneasiness forming in the pit of my stomach. Am I overrating ace-jack?

——THE TURN——

Loose Guy checks to me again.

Forget about this being a critical spot in the hand: My whole tournament is on the line. If I invest any more money into this pot, I will likely be pot committed.

I have decidedly mixed feelings about the jack on the turn. The good news is it gave me two pair. Given the size of the pot in relation to my stack, I have to consider moving all-in. The bad news is that I still can't be sure he's not slowplaying a monster. An all-in bet here could send me packing.

What would you do?

I still think there is a very good possibility that I'm significantly in the lead here, but given how coordinated the board has become—there are two different flush draws and all kinds of straight possibilities—I have to bet. I'm not going to give him a free card . . . but do I have to risk all of my chips?

My best bet, so to speak, might be a compromise. If I bet about three quarters of the pot, somewhere around $15,000, I should be able to close out most of his draws, as I'll only be giving him around 2.5–1 on his money.

I push $15,000 into the middle with some trepidation.

Loose Guy squints as he studies the board. He

looks at his cards again. He looks at the board again. He shuffles his cards, seemingly poised to throw them away, then:

"Well, if I'm going to go broke, at least I can tell my friends that Phil Gordon busted me."

I am suddenly aware of the cameras around me. So, as it seems, is he.

"I'm all-in," Loose Guy continues. "You want me to count it?"

What would you do?

I don't need a chip count. I already know that calling him is going to force me to risk the rest of my stack. I'm asked to call my last $15,000 to win an $80,000 pot. If I'm behind, I have six outs and a 12% chance to make my hand on the river. I'm not getting the right odds to call off all my chips . . . if I'm behind.

But this hand isn't about math anymore: It's about psychology. I am nearly certain that I'm behind. When a player takes the time to make a speech at the table, that almost always means it's time to get out of his way. I learned this little tell several years ago from the great T. J. Cloutier, and it has rarely disappointed me.

"Nice hand," I say, throwing my cards into the

muck. I don't really mean it. A few months from now, when I see the broadcast on ESPN, I pray that commentator Norman Chad will be saying something like, "Oh, boy, Phil Gordon was in more trouble on that hand than my third ex-wife after I caught her with the plumber. I have no *idea* how he escaped."

For now I'll remind myself that I'm still alive, I have fifteen big blinds, and its time to get very aggressive.

❧ KEY ANALYSIS ❧

Beware of the speech. The speech is almost always accompanied by a strong hand. Don't ignore evidence and make a quick, automatic call. Trust your instincts and reads.

BAD POSITION

THE SITUATION: Day two of a major tournament. About seventy players remain.

—NO LIMIT HOLD'EM TOURNAMENT—

Blinds $5,000/$10,000 with $1,000 antes

POT: $54,000   **TO CALL:** $25,000   **POT ODDS:** 2.2–1

Dan Harrington has a reputation for being a very tight poker player. Of course, he knows exactly what people think of him, and he exploits his image to pick spots to steal blinds during the middle and late stages of a tournament.

Regardless of whether or not he's trying to steal here, I'm getting decent odds to call, unless I'm up against A-A, A-K, K-K, or Q-Q.

What would you do?

152

Against a loose player, I'd be inclined to re-raise here. A-Q is a good hand but not one I want to play out of position against a preflop raiser. When I'm out of position, I like to win the pot before the flop whenever possible.

Against Dan, however, I'm much less willing to get involved with this hand. Having to act first is a huge disadvantage. I'd really have to flop a monster hand to feel comfortable playing from bad position against a great player. And even if I do flop a huge hand, what are the odds that "Action Dan" is going to pay me off? Slim to none.

Maybe I'm falling victim to his image, but there are many "softer spots" at this table than Dan Harrington. Poker is about picking your spots. And playing an easily dominated hand from bad position against a tight-aggressive world champion doesn't seem like one of them.

I fold and wait for a better situation. And yes, I know Dan had T-4 offsuit that hand. I just know it.

❧ KEY ANALYSIS ❧

There's no rule that says you have to play a very good or even great hand when it's dealt to you. If you don't like the spot you're in, fold the hand and wait for another, more profitable situation.

SHORT-STACKED

THE SITUATION: The middle rounds of a $500 buy-in tournament. Around fifty-five players remain. The average stack is about $30,000.

──NO LIMIT HOLD'EM TOURNAMENT──
Blinds $500/$1,000 with $100 antes

POT: $6,400   **TO CALL:** $3,500   **POT ODDS:** 1.8–1

While I'm not on life support yet, with just thirteen big blinds I'm getting damn near close. My focus is on finding a spot to get all of my chips into the middle while (1) I still have enough chips to cause an opponent to think twice before calling my bet, and (2) doubling up will leave me with something resembling an average stack.

What would you do?

From where I'm sitting—behind a very small pile of chips—I can't really ask for a situation much better than this one:

♦ There has been a raise in front of me, which has built a pot that is worth targeting. Even if he folds, I'll add more than six big blinds to my stack.

♦ The preflop raiser is a loose-aggressive player who may very well be on a steal.

♦ He has a slightly above-average stack: not so big that he doesn't mind taking a risk, and not so small that he *has* to take a risk.

♦ There is only one player left to act behind me, which minimizes the chance that I run into a monster hand.

♦ I have a pretty good hand. I'm favored to beat anything other than aces, kings, or queens.

This one is a no-brainer. I push all-in. He beats me to the pot and turns over A♥A♦.

——THE FLOP——

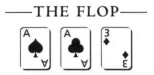

My chances have diminished, er, *considerably*. I don't need to see the last two cards—they can't possibly help me—and I'm on my way out the door. Regardless of the outcome, however, I stand by my play, and I'd do it again. There are some situations that occur at the table where you just can't help but go broke.

——❖ KEY ANALYSIS ❖——

When your stack dwindles to thirteen to fifteen big blinds or so, look for spots to push all-in, ideally from the blinds against a loose-aggressive raiser. Don't get blinded off. Take a stand while you have a shot of doubling up and getting back to average.

SHORT-STACKED AGAIN

THE SITUATION: The middle rounds of a tournament. Around fifty players remain. The average stack is about $30,000.

──NO LIMIT HOLD'EM TOURNAMENT──
Blinds $500/$1,000 with $100 antes

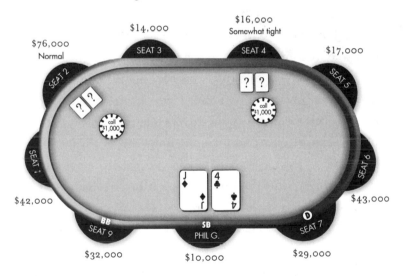

POT: $4,400   TO CALL: $500   POT ODDS: 8.8–1

Once again I find myself on the short stack with only ten big blinds remaining. The J-4 offsuit I've been dealt isn't much, but I'm getting incredible pot odds to call. I have a few options here: Call from the small blind and invest $500 of my remaining $10,000, or I can really take a stand and push all-in.

What would you do?

At first glance this might seem like an easy call. Assuming the big blind doesn't raise, I'm getting nearly 9–1 odds on my $500 investment. Against three random hands J-4 stands to win around 20% of the time, making this a correct money decision.

But these aren't likely to be "normal" hands. At this point in the tournament my opponents are far more likely to be playing better-than-average hands, more than a few of which may have me dominated. If I call here, I'll have no idea what to do if I flop a pair against three other players. Unless I flop two pair, trips, or a straight, which will happen less than 5% of the time, I'll likely be faced with some ridiculously difficult decisions.

It is clear that there are better opportunities to gamble with my limited funds. I save my money and fold.

Playing speculative hands with small positive equity makes sense in a cash game or a tournament when you are deep stacked. When your stack gets short, however, you are better off saving the money and using it later to exert maximum pressure.

A SCARE CARD HITS THE TURN

THE SITUATION: The middle rounds of a $100 buy-in tournament on FullTiltPoker.com. About one hundred players remain. The average stack is around $6,000.

$7,950
Intermediate

$7,450

$6,900

DOWNLOWE
SB

THETODD
BB

$18,500

BIGLAW

CIRCUSBEAR

MARTYS
NEPHEW

IRISHMAN

$3,000

$9,800

JUSTPAT

PHIL G.

BROWNIE

$2,200

$5,500

$1,600

POT: $240   **TO CALL:** $160   **POT ODDS:** 1.5–1

I stop surfing the web immediately and give the hand my full attention, of course. Pocket Rockets, and they couldn't come at a better time.

What would you do?

I see no reason to vary from my normal aggressive strategy. From middle position I'll open with a standard raise, three times the big blind.

I raise to $480. I'm mildly disappointed when everyone folds, until DownLowe, in the small blind, opts to call. There is $1,120 in the pot.

——THE FLOP——

DownLowe checks to me.

I do not like to slowplay in this situation. I seriously doubt she's called me with anything that has straight potential here, but there is a flush draw out there and I don't have the A♥. I'm going to bet. The only question is, how much? What would you do?

I bet the pot, $1,120. I don't think the size of the bet will scare her into folding a pair of tens, and she's going to have to think long and hard before calling with a flush draw.

DownLowe takes her time and then calls my bet, creating a pot of $3,360.

When I bet and a good player calls—especially when she's getting incorrect odds to chase any kind of draw—I start to sweat.

—THE TURN—

That's an ugly card for me. If she was calling with some kind of flush draw, she just got there. If she's already in front of me—a set is a definite possibility, given her big call on the flop—this card hasn't done anything to improve my situation.

DownLowe checks to me, and I'm faced with another tough decision. What would you do?

When a scare card hits the turn and my opponent checks to me, I usually check behind her.

I'm actually torn between competing impulses here. On the one hand, I want to protect my hand with a bet; I don't want to check and see a fourth heart on the river. On the other hand, there is more than $3,000 in the pot, about half an average stack. If I bet any more here, I am going to be dangerously close to committing myself to this pot.

After quite a bit of mental flip-flopping, I finally decide to check. The speed with which she called the flop leads me to believe she had a flush draw, and thus, now a flush. I could be completely wrong, but if indeed there are eight hearts left in the deck, the Rule of Two tells me that there's only about a 16% chance of a fourth heart appearing on the river. I'd rather take that risk than put myself in a position to go broke with this hand.

——THE RIVER——

DownLowe leads out with a $1,000 bet. There is $4,360 in the pot, and it will cost me $1,000 to call.

After playing the turn like a wimp, I think I have to call this $1,000 bet. I'm not happy about it, of course, and I'm definitely not at all interested in raising with my medium-strength hand.

I call. She turns over 6♥5♥, having flopped a pair and a flush draw, and rakes in more than $5,000.

I'm bitter, of course, but cognizant that I could have lost a lot more. I made a good read on the turn and avoided total disaster.

Now let me go cry in the corner for a while.

❧ KEY ANALYSIS ❧

When a scare card hits the turn, it's often okay to relinquish the lead to your opponent. And do your best not to go broke with one pair!

THE WAITING IS THE HARDEST PART

THE SITUATION: The middle rounds of a tournament. Around one hundred fifty players remain. The average stack is about $5,000. The blinds are scheduled to increase, from $100/$200 to $200/$400, on the next hand.

——NO LIMIT HOLD'EM TOURNAMENT——
Blinds $100/$200

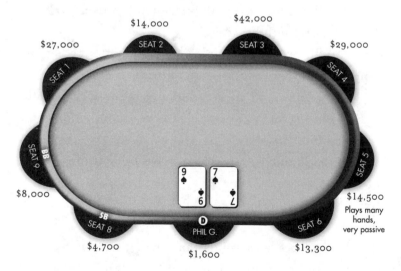

POT: $300 **TO CALL:** $200 **POT ODDS:** 1.5–1

With only eight big blinds left I am gasping for oxygen. I have to find spots to push all-in, hopefully stealing the blinds from the average stacks (or doubling up, should they call). At first glance this seems like one of those spots.

Is this the time to gamble? What would you do?

A second glance—this time at the tournament clock, which tells me that the blinds are going to double on the next hand—leads me to rethink my position. Why risk everything on a marginal hand to win $300, when on the very next hand I'll have a chance to play for $600?

I know that the increase in blinds will decrease my relative standing from eight big blinds to just four. But I'll have six more hands to find a similarly reasonable (if not a much better) hand that I can play with twice the potential upside.

I fold here and hope for a better spot.

❖ KEY ANALYSIS ❖

When you're on a short stack and the blinds are about to increase, it's often more profitable to wait for a spot to steal the bigger blinds than to take a shot at the smaller blinds with a marginal hand.

ACCEPTING DONATIONS

THE SITUATION: The late middle of a tournament. About one hundred twenty players remain. The average stack is about $40,000.

──NO LIMIT HOLD'EM TOURNAMENT──
Blinds $1,000/$2,000 with $300 antes

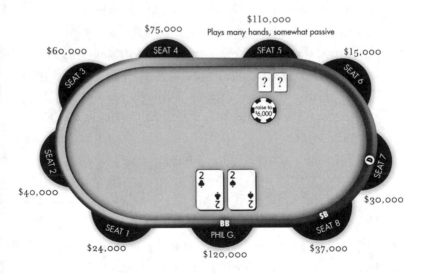

POT: $11,700   **TO CALL:** $4,000   **POT ODDS:** 2.9–1

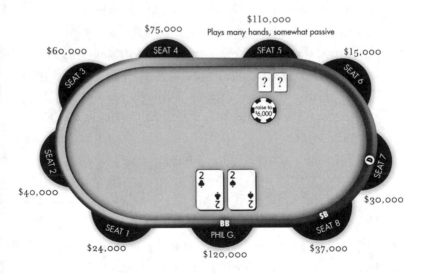

I love to play pocket pairs in No Limit Hold'em tournaments. If you can see the flop relatively cheaply, they are the ultimate in low-risk, high-reward opportunities. You either flop a set—and hopefully drag a huge pot—or miss and fold without investing any more money. Note that the "you hit it or you don't" strategy also negates any positional disadvantage you might face going into the hand.

In this particular situation the preflop raise means that I'm not getting such a cheap look at the flop. I'm only going to flop a set or better about 12% of the time, meaning that I'd technically need pot odds of 7.5–1 or better to play my 2-2. The real value of pocket pairs, however, comes from the *implied* pot odds: My opponent won't know that I've flopped a set, and I'll hopefully have a shot at separating him from a large number of chips. As a result, any time I'm relatively deep stacked (forty big blinds or more) and my opponent has enough chips to pay me off in a big way should I flop my set, I'll call up to five big blinds with any pocket pair.

An added bonus here: My opponent is loose and passive, which means my implied odds are higher than normal. He's more likely to call my bets with a wide range of (hopefully losing) hands.

I call his raise. There is $15,700 in the pot.

——THE FLOP——

Yes! When I flop a set out of position, I immediately evaluate the board to determine the likelihood that my opponent has flopped top pair or an overpair. If it's unlikely, as it is in this case, I'll usually check my hand, allowing him a chance to bluff now or catch a pair on the turn.

Against a calling station, however, I don't want to miss a chance to bet. I want him to call me with A-K or 8-8. If he has one of those hands, I can imagine him calling up to a third of the pot. If I bet more, I risk snapping the line and letting my big fish get away.

I bet $5,000. He calls. There is $25,700 in the pot.

——THE TURN——

There's still no reason to scare him off yet, but straight and flush draws are starting to percolate, so I want to err on the side of caution and not risk giving him correct odds to call if he does have a draw. With that in mind I look to bet a little more than a third of the pot, giving him just under 4–1 odds to call.

I bet $10,000. He calls. There is $45,700 in the pot.

——THE RIVER——

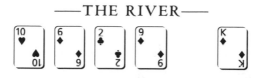

I know there are possible straights on the board, and there is a chance that he has been slowplaying a bigger set than mine. Against many players I'd probably resist the urge to bet the river here. My set seemed like a monster on the flop. Now it's looking more vulnerable.

Against a calling station, however, I will make more money betting winning hands on the river than I will save by checking my losing hands. A hand like A-K would be not only consistent with his betting patterns but ideal for me should he decide to call. Once again, keeping my opponent's likely holdings in mind, I try to dial in a number that maximizes my return (assuming, of course, that I'm right.) Here I feel that the right number is half the pot.

I bet $25,000. "I should raise you," says my opponent as he calls my bet. I smile politely as I turn over my three deuces. "Or maybe not," he chuckles as he throws big slick into the muck.

❖ KEY ANALYSIS ❖

Against a calling station, slowplaying and bluffing are rarely profitable plays. You will make your money against this player by pounding him with value bet after value bet.

TO HELL WITH THE DEVIL

THE SITUATION: The second day of a three-day $3,000 buy-in tournament. A few hundred players remain. The average stack is about $40,000.

POT: $5,700   **TO CALL:** $2,000   **POT ODDS:** 2.9–1

I have a theory about what a poker game in hell might look like: You'd be under the gun on every single hand, against a table full of aggressive professionals. And you'd be holding pocket jacks.

No other hand causes players—even the most seasoned pros—so much agitation. Nearly a 3.5–1 favorite over two random cards, they are a great hand to raise with . . . unless someone decides to call your raise. Even if your opponent doesn't have you dominated with a bigger pocket pair, more than half of the flops you see will include at least one overcard to your jacks. Simply stated, pocket jacks will force you to make some very difficult decisions.

So, here we are in hell. What would you do?

There is no way in hell I'm going to dump this hand before the flop. Both of the blinds have average stacks, I've got a good table image, and I've got two matching face cards. I'm playing. And since I'm the first to the pot, I'm coming in for a raise.

I raise to $5,000. One by one they all fold. I'm thrilled. When we get to the button, however, Dave "the Devilfish" Ulliott re-raises to $15,000. The Devilfish wears more jewelry than a gangsta rapper, some of which, I'm sure, was paid for with the small fortune I've lost to him in cash games. He is one of the trickiest players in the world. He'll hit on your girlfriend by whispering sweet nothings in her ear . . . while you're standing next to her. Needless to say, he'll triple your under-the-gun raise without hesitation if he thinks he can buy the pot.

There is $25,700 in the pot, and it will cost me another $10,000 to call. There we have it, folks . . . this is why we hate pocket jacks.

Here's what I know: The Devil (we'll lose the "fish" for the sake of metaphor) is a superaggressive player, but he respects my game. There are plenty of legitimate hands he'd re-raise me with: A-A, K-K, Q-Q, and A-K are all possibilities. I'm pretty sure he'd just smooth-call my raise with a lower pocket pair or A-Q. But, if he sensed weakness, he might monkey around with a subpremium hand. Given that he's an expert and I'm on pocket jacks, there might just be a hint of Uncertainty (a yet-to-be released perfume by Calvin Klein) in the air.

What would you do?

If you're not a big fan of math, you may want to skip this next part.

Assuming I call the bet, there will be $35,700 in the pot. Against A-A, K-K, or Q-Q, I'll only win about 20% of the time. My expected return in these situations is 20% of $35,700, or $7,140.

Against A-K, I'll win about 57% of the time. My expected return in these situations is 57% of $35,700, or $20,349.

There are eighteen ways he could have A-A, K-K, or Q-Q, and sixteen ways he could have A-K. In other words I'm facing one of thirty-four different combinations of cards.

About 53% of the time (18÷34) he'll have a big pocket pair, and I can expect to win $7,140. That's 53% x $7,140, or $3,784 in expected return.

The other 47% of the time he'll have A-K, and I can expect to win $20,349. That's 47% x $20,349, or $9,564 in expected return.

My expected average return in *all* of these situations is $3,784 + $9,564, or $13,348.

I am being asked to invest another $10,000 into this pot. I can expect to make about $13,348. In other words, calling here should show a modest profit.

There are other variables, of course. These odds are based on a showdown where we get to see all five community cards. That's not likely to happen. We've also used the money currently in the pot to make our calculations, discounting any potential for money to be added later in the hand, something that is very likely to happen. If he's bluffing, all of my math goes out the window. In theory, however, I believe that calling in this position is, by a slim margin, the correct course of action. If you fold your preflop raises from this position too often, your opponents will never respect your raises and will run right over you.

I call. There is $35,700 in the pot, and I have about $40,000 left.

——THE FLOP——

I'm either a poker genius or the Devil has pocket aces and I'm about to have a bad-beat story to tell. The only hand he could have (other than pocket aces) that would give him any decent chance to win is A♦K♦. If he's got anything else, he's drawing nearly dead.

Should I bet? Check, with the intention of slow-playing?

What would you do?

Well, I'm not about to worry about set over set. If he's flopped a set with pocket aces, I'm willing to go broke. If I win this very large pot, I'll have the chip lead at my table and I'll have nearly double the average stack.

Assuming I do have the best hand, how can I get the most out of the Devil? If he has K-K or Q-Q, I don't think he'll bet very much if I check to him. He'll be afraid that I have an ace. I certainly don't want to give him a free card to catch up. If he's holding A-K, he's probably going to call whatever bet I make.

I decide to make the maximum move and go all-in. If I scare him off, so be it. As I said, this pot is already big enough to dramatically improve my tournament prospects.

After debating for a few minutes, the Devil decides to call me with A♦K♥. My set of jacks holds up to win, and I'm catapulted into the chip lead. If hell is pocket jacks under the gun, then heaven must be hitting a set and doubling up into the chip lead.

◈ KEY ANALYSIS ◈

Deciding how to play pocket jacks can be extremely difficult. You'll be forced to make some very, very difficult decisions. Ultimately, math, consideration of all the variables of that particular hand, and experience will help you make the right choices.

A GUINNESS TO THE GENIUS

THE SITUATION: The middle stages of a weekly $500 buy-in multitable tournament at the Bellagio. About eighty players remain. The average stack is about $25,000.

—NO LIMIT HOLD'EM TOURNAMENT—
Blinds $500/$1,000

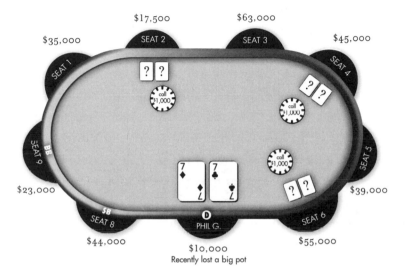

POT: $4,500   **TO CALL:** $1,000   **POT ODDS:** 4.5–1

Things have not been going my way: I've taken a couple of brutal bad beats in the last fifteen minutes. But I'm still clear, focused, and intent on playing my best.

When I'm in late position and several players limp into the pot, my first instinct is to raise. After all, how great a hand is a limper likely to have?

I also know that with a hand like 7-7, the real value comes from the implied odds should I flop a set. In other words, I want to see a cheap flop, preferably against a lot

177

of other players. This will increase the odds that I can double up on one of them if I spike a seven on the flop.

So, what's the right play? Do I raise the limpers, or do I call cheaply and hope to flop a set?

What would you do?

In this particular scenario both options are trumped by a third course of action that accounts for an even more important factor: I am short stacked. With only ten big blinds, I am looking for an all-or-nothing situation that will put me back into contention. I've found a good one here.

If I can get everyone to fold, I'll take a decent pot without a showdown, increase my stack by almost 50%, and carve out a little more breathing room.

How good are the hands that my opponents are likely to have? An all-in raise from me is going to force them to gamble a significant amount of money if they want to take a fifty-fifty shot. If they were willing to gamble that kind of money with the cards they're holding, they probably would have entered the pot with a raise. Remember, ten big blinds (or, in this case, $10,000) is a significant amount of chips—nearly half an average stack!

Of course someone could be slowplaying a monster hand, or decide that it's worth calling me with an A-9 or K-Q. If so, I'll be getting pot odds of better than 1.3–1. Those are great odds for a coin flip. Just imagine someone offered to pay you $1.30 every time the coin came up heads, but only charged you $1 when the coin came up tails. This is the kind of gamble I like: A proposition with high positive equity.*

Raising all-in seems like the best play, and I do just that. Everyone folds to Seat 6, who decides to call with A-T offsuit.

"You on tilt there, Mr. Gordon?" he asks. At least he called me "Mr. Gordon." I survive the flop and the turn, but he catches a ten on the river to eliminate me.

"Now I am," I respond as I collect my jacket and head for the bar.

Well, as the great philosopher Kurtis Blow once observed, "These are the breaks." Instead of getting blinded off, I got my money into the middle of a situation in a great spot. The cold pint of Guinness in my hand provides some solace. I know I made the right play; I just got the wrong result.

◆ K E Y   A N A L Y S I S ◆

A short stack + Lots of limpers = Good time to push all-in with any hand that has a decent chance of winning a showdown.

---

* If I had the same hand and an average stack, I would not raise all-in. I'd just call and hope to flop a set against many players. The implied odds associated with flopping a set are much higher than the pot odds I get from moving all-in.

FOUR ACES

THE SITUATION: The middle stages of a $1,500 buy-in tournament at Caesars Palace, Las Vegas. About one hundred players remain. The average stack is about $65,000.

——NO LIMIT HOLD'EM TOURNAMENT——
Blinds $1,000/$2,000 with $100 antes

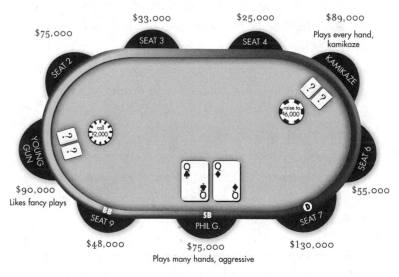

POT: $11,900 **TO CALL:** $5,000 **POT ODDS:** 2.4–1

I've been splashing around the pot lately, hence my notated loose-aggressive image. But this time, like my time spent as a bartender at Club Med, I've got the ladies. As for the young kid prone to making fancy plays who limped in under the gun—no big deal. I've seen him do that before with 7-6 suited. A raise from Kamikaze in Seat 5 doesn't mean much either, although it is a suspiciously small raise.

When someone raises in front of my great hand, there are several factors I like to consider before I act.

What are the arguments for re-raising?

♣ Position, or, in this case, lack thereof. I am much more likely to re-raise than call in this situation, in order to negate my positional disadvantage. From the blinds, I like to win the pot before the flop when possible.

♣ They're just queens. An ace or a king is going to hit the flop about 35% of the time. Like most people, I hate pain, and in Hold'em there aren't many situations more painful than leading out with queens into a flop with an ace and/or a king against an opponent who has called your preflop raise.

♣ If I call, I'm almost guaranteed to have three-way action. By re-raising I can limit my competition and most likely face only a single opponent (or, hopefully, zero opponents).

What are the arguments for just calling?

♥ I can get in relatively cheaply, see if I flop a set against two players, and maintain my above-average stack. If an ace or king flops, I can just check/fold and still have a good shot at winning the tournament. If my queens turn out to be an overpair to the flop, I'm going to be committed to playing the hand and investing a significant number of chips.

♥ If I re-raise and one of these yahoos pushes all-in, I'm going to be in a very, very tough situation. I'm particularly worried about Kamikaze making a big play.

What would you do? Call or re-raise? If you decide to re-raise, how much?

I eventually opt to re-raise. I'd rather give myself a shot to win the pot before the flop because I'm out of position. I like to re-raise about three or four times the size of my opponent's bet. Since Kamikaze came in for three times the big blind, I'll make it nine.

I re-raise to $18,000. That's when the fireworks start.

Young Gun suddenly comes to life, re-raising to

$40,000. Kamikaze re-raises all-in. The action is on me.

Before I go into my usual routine (evaluating the probable strength of my opponents' hands, calculating pot odds, puking, adjusting for the probability of a three-way pot, blah, blah, blah), there's a simple poker truism that past experience has taught me to never disregard:

The fourth raise before the flop means pocket aces.

There aren't any certainties in poker, but this one is pretty close. If these guys are daredevil pilots ready to crash-and-burn with something less than "American Airlines," well, they got me to fold a great hand. But I'll like my chances of getting their chips soon.

At best I'm playing pocket queens for all of my chips in a three-way pot, where I'm probably a huge underdog. I'll happily fold here and wait for clearer skies. This seems like a good time for a bathroom break. I don't need to see how this one plays out.

❖ KEY ANALYSIS ❖

The fourth raise almost always means pocket aces.

ROCKET MAN

THE SITUATION: The middle stages of a small buy-in tournament. About one hundred players remain. The average stack is about $60,000.

——NO LIMIT HOLD'EM TOURNAMENT——
Blinds $1,000/$2,000 with $100 antes

$33,000 — SEAT 3
$25,000 — SEAT 4
$75,000 — SEAT 2
$89,000 — SEAT 5
SEAT 1
raise to $8,000
? ?
SHORTY
$90,000
$10,000
BB — SEAT 9
SB — PHIL G.
D — SEAT 7
$84,000
$55,000
$130,000

POT: $11,900   **TO CALL:** $7,000   **POT ODDS:** 1.7–1

This is my first hand at a new table, and I don't recognize a soul. Nor does anyone acknowledge me as I take my seat. Maybe they don't watch *Celebrity Poker Showdown*. "Must not be Dave Folcy fans," I say to myself.

I'm whipped out of my little internal monologue the moment I look at my cards. Yes! My first hand at a new table, I get Pocket Rockets, and there's action to boot. Perfect! I couldn't be more thrilled.

When the poker gods smile on me and deal me bullets, the question isn't whether or not to play but how to get my opponents to risk as much money as possible.

I have two options at this point:

1. Re-raise and isolate. There's little doubt that the pre-flop raiser will call his last $10,000, as he'll be getting almost 3—1 on his money.
2. Call and hope to "trap" my opponent after the flop. Doing so will give the big blind behind me fairly decent odds to call, but (in a perfect world) it might induce him to try an isolation raise of his own.

What would you do?

The devil on my shoulder is screaming into my ear: "Just call! Try to suck in the big blind!" As a general rule, however, I ignore the devil unless I'm in Amsterdam.

It's clear that a re-raise is the better play:

♠ Calling gives the big blind pretty decent odds to follow me into the pot. I don't want the big blind to call. Playing pocket aces against a single opponent, I'm (likely to be) a one-man wrecking crew. Playing them against two or more opponents, there's a much better chance of getting wrecked.

♠ I'm out of position. Let's say Shorty is holding 9-9 and the flop comes A-K-J. What are the odds that he puts another dime into the pot? Or what if the flop brings 9-8-7 with three spades. Would *I* want to put another dime into the pot? Once we see the cards, there are all kinds of scenarios that might get him to chicken out and save the last $10,000. Putting him all-in before the flop cures those problems.

♠ I've already got him on the hook! This is, far and away, the best argument for re-raising all-in right now. He's risked nearly half his stack on this hand, and will be getting about 3–1 odds to call my all-in raise. Unless he's sure that I'm holding a bigger pocket pair than he is, there's no way he can fold to my raise. I may have some tells—at least according to Mike Matusow—but I'm not *completely* transparent. No, for sure he's going to call.

I re-raise to $20,000. No reason to move all-in here. If the big blind finds A-K or Q-Q, I definitely want him to play, and I want it to look like I'm trying to isolate Shorty.

The big blind folds, and Shorty calls instantly with A-K. The board fails to help him. As he rises from his seat to take the long walk of shame, he snarls over his shoulder: "Gordon, you really should look for a better job. . . . Bravo? And tell Dave Foley to lay off the Scotch."

Turns out we do have a fan after all!

❌ K E Y   A N A L Y S I S ❌

Keep an eye on your opponents' stacks. When they've put more than half their chips into a pot, they're usually committed to risking the rest. Choose your actions accordingly.

LATE TOURNAMENT PLAY

If the pressure starts to build during a tournament's middle stages, it gets thicker than pea soup during the later rounds. The primary culprit for all of this tension: the approaching bubble. No one wants to be the player who finishes one spot away from the money. The tight players get tighter, desperate players get more desperate, and the great players take advantage of both.

At this point the players still in the tournament will generally fall into two categories. Conservative players will look to hold on to their chips, knowing that all they

have to do for a payday is outlast a few of their opponents. Aggressive players—and I am guilty as charged—will
search out opportunities to put pressure on the conservative players, taking advantage of their unwillingness to
take big risks without big hands.

I don't play tournaments to squeak into the money.
I play tournaments to win. As a result, this is my make-
or-break time. I am still going to be selective in my
aggression, but I am willing to take a lot more chances.
I am usually looking to build a very large stack—one that
will give me the best chance of winning—or I'll go broke
trying.

ADIOS, AMIGOS

THE SITUATION: Day three of the 2001 *WSOP*
$10,000 No Limit Hold'em championship. Thirteen
players remain on two tables.

Blinds $3,000 /$6,000 with $1,000 antes

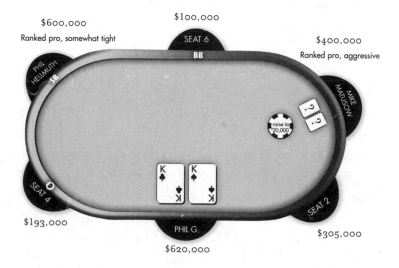

$600,000
Ranked pro, somewhat tight

$100,000

SEAT 6

BB

$400,000
Ranked pro, aggressive

PHIL HELLMUTH $SB

MIKE MATUSOW

raise to 20,000

? ?

K♠ K♣

SEAT 4 D

$193,000

PHIL G.

$620,000

SEAT 2

$305,000

POT: $35,000 **TO CALL:** $20,000 **POT ODDS:** 1.8–1

Yep . . . it's the *World Series of Poker*, the biggest tournament in the world. We started with 613 players, and there are 13 left. I can just about see the final table—if I squint hard, that is. And now I've just woken up with the second-best starting hand in Texas Hold'em.

I have to be a little concerned that Mike Matusow, an expert player known for his aggressiveness, has opened for a big raise, a little more than three times the size of the big blind. It's not going to stop me, however, from playing this hand and playing it aggressively. We're six-handed and Mike has been playing a lot of hands. He's also talking incessantly. Imagine that. His raise doesn't necessarily mean he has a big hand. No doubt about it, I am going to play this hand. The only decision I have to make is simple: call or re-raise.

What would you do?

Just calling here seems like bad business, as I'll be giving the players in the blinds (specifically, Phil Hellmuth Jr.) better than 3–to–1 odds to join the pot. Pocket kings are a very powerful hand heads-up, but I'm going to lose a lot of equity if I give the other players such a juicy invitation to make a big score. I'm going to re-raise in an effort to isolate the initial raiser.

But how much to re-raise? One thing I have to consider is that "The Mouth" is more experienced and skilled than I am. I don't want to get outplayed after the flop, especially if an ace appears (something that will happen around 17% of the time). If he's holding A-K or A-Q, I'd be more than happy to take the pot down right here before the flop: I'd extend my chip lead at the table and avoid a big confrontation. A substantial re-raise from me might have the added effect of convincing him that I don't want a call here, leading him to push all-in against me with a small or medium pocket pair. I will, without hesitation, call Mike if he moves all-in as a response to my re-raise.

So, my decision is made: I'm going to re-raise. Now, the second important decision: How much?

How much would you re-raise?

I settle on my number, a nice round number. Six figures. I announce the re-raise and slide $100,000 into the pot. My mom, sitting in the audience, gasps audibly. I know my hands are shaking.

I'm concentrating so hard on Matusow, trying to pick up a read, that I completely forget that Phil Hellmuth Jr. in is the small blind—black hat, jacket zipped up to the top, headphones on. Intensely focused, he pauses for just a few seconds before moving all-in, about $600,000. The big blind folds very quickly. After agonizing for a minute or so, Matusow folds as well.* There is $735,000 in the pot, and it's going to cost me another $500,000 to call.

What would you do?

I can feel my hands, as if they have a mind of their

---

* It turns out Mike, who had pocket queens, made a pretty good laydown of his own!

own, moving my chips toward the center of the table. Were this my Wednesday night home game against the Tiltboys, I'd push all-in without a second thought. Unless Hellmuth has pocket aces, I'm a huge favorite to win a huge pot (and knock him out of the tournament in the process.) But against the Tiltboys, I could lose the hand (a bad beat from Dave "Diceboy" Lambert, no doubt) and reach back into my wallet for more money. This is the *World Series,* and I might never get this close to the final table again. I take a deep breath and think this through again.

One of the most important reasons to raise before the flop is to force your opponents to define their hands. That's what I was doing when I raised Matusow. And that's what Hellmuth has done by putting all of his chips on the line against two players who have already represented strength.

What do I think of Hellmuth? He's arrogant, but for good reason: He's one of the best No Limit tournament players in the history of the game. Phil Hellmuth Jr. has been in situations like this before. It's very unlikely that he's making an impulsive decision here. He's made difficult laydowns in the past, and wouldn't have any trouble throwing a hand like pocket jacks or queens into the muck in the face of a raise and re-raise.

He's not in any danger of getting blinded out of this tournament anytime soon, so he's under no pressure to "make a play" here. He's got to like his chances against this lineup. And he knows I'm getting excellent odds to gamble with him here.

What does he think of me? Probably not very much. When you know you're one of the best players in the world, everyone else is just a speed bump. I just happen to be a taller speed bump than most. He can't be sure that I'm going to be "smart" enough to throw my hand away, so he's almost certainly not bluffing. The only thing that might piss him off more than losing would be to look like an idiot, which he certainly might if he happened to get caught running a bluff against two players at this stage in the tournament. In other words, he's risking not only almost all of his chips on this play but also his reputation.

He must not think I have a better hand than he has. That leaves only one possibility—he has pocket aces.

Am I certain? Yes, as certain as I've ever been of anything at the poker table. This may be the biggest lay-down of my lifetime, but all the signs point to this decision. I pull my hands away from my remaining stack and toss my cards into the muck.

"Nice hand," I say.

"What'd you have, Gordon, ace-queen?" snickers the other Phil.

"Nope. Just two kings."

I fish them out of the muck to prove it to him. He doesn't smile as he turns over his pocket aces. That's okay. I'm grinning wide enough for both of us, and my mom is proud.

"I'm so unlucky," he moans. "I mean, I've got aces against queens and kings on the same hand and all I can win is a hundred grand."

Yes, Phil, you're unlucky.

❖ KEY ANALYSIS ❖

Instincts and judgment aren't enough; you need the discipline and courage to act decisively.

MARCO POLO

———◆———

THE SITUATION: Day two of the 2005 *WSOP* $2,000 Pot-Limit Hold'em championship. About twenty-seven players remain at three tables.

$17,500

$63,000

$45,000

$39,000

SEAT 2

SEAT 3

SEAT 4

SEAT 5

SEAT 1

SEAT 6

$35,000

$55,000

BB
MARCO
TRANIELLO

SB
PHIL G.

D

SEAT 7

$48,000

$44,000

$13,000

Expert

POT: $4,200   **TO CALL:** $800   **POT ODDS:** 5.3–1

I hate playing hands out of the small blind. I am confident that I have lost much, much more money than I have won playing hands from the small blind, where I am guaranteed to be in bad position. Yes, position is that important.

With everyone folding to me, it's decision time: call or raise. What would you do?

I'm certainly not going to fold A-T here. I don't *have* to make a move. With nearly thirty big blinds in my stack, I have plenty of time. That said, the odds are that my hand is better than whatever two random cards my friend Marco Traniello happens to be holding behind me.

I like to raise to three times the big blind in this spot, enough to drive out a weak hand. I'd be more than happy to take the $4,200 on the table without a contest. I make it $4,800 and I think this is the right amount.

Marco calls. There is $11,400 in the pot, and already I have a bad feeling in my stomach. So much for stealing the blinds. Not only have I been called, but I've been called by Marco, who has been on a tear at the World Series this year. . . . He's already cashed in five of the first fifteen events.

——THE FLOP——

Good news, bad news. The good news is that I've flopped middle pair (with an excellent kicker), a very strong hand against a single opponent. The bad news is that the cards are closely grouped, creating all kinds of straight and two pair possibilities.

Should I bet or check? What would you do?

Checking doesn't seem right, given the dangerous texture of the board. I can't afford to give Marco a free card here, and if I check and show weakness and he bets the pot, I'll have no idea what to do. Another reason to bet: My hand is unlikely to improve. There are only five cards left in the deck that can help me.

Normally I'd make a good-size bet here, maybe two thirds the size of the pot, in the hopes of taking down the hand right now. But do I really want to commit one fourth of my stack, out of position, with middle pair?

What if I made a smaller bet? If I bet around half of the pot, he won't be getting the right odds to pursue most draws, and if he comes over the top of me, I can think about folding.

Maybe it's too conservative, but I decide to bet $5,000.

Marco calls after some thought, and there is now $21,400 in the pot. I hate my hand.

——THE TURN——

Okay, I'm officially terrified. I've bet enough to scare off most draws, but Marco—a good player whose game I respect—has just called. Alarm bells are going off in my head. There is a very serious possibility I'm up against a monster hand.

But what monster hands could he have? An overpair? He probably would have re-raised me before the flop. Did he flop a set? Also unlikely. Board texture is a double-edged sword. He's got to fear the straight draw as well and surely would have raised my bet on the flop to protect his hand had he flopped three of a kind, or even two pair.

His call seems to indicate that he's not afraid of the straight. Either he's holding J-9 (in which case I'm drawing pretty much dead), or he's got a hand like Q-J, J-T, T-9, Q-9, J-8, or 9-8: a pair with straight possibilities. Marco is perfectly capable of calling my pre-flop raise with those hands because he knows he'll be in position.

The biggest problem is that I've allowed this pot to get too big. While I'm not quite pot committed, that $21,400 in the pot sure would look good in my stack. If I check here, Marco will almost certainly use his position to bet and take the pot away from me.

What would you do? Bet or check?

I think my only chance of winning is to remain aggressive. I'll fire another bet—one third of the pot or so—to protect myself against a draw, and pray that he folds. Should he call or raise me, I'm probably beat.

I bet $8,000. Marco mulls again and finally calls. There is $37,400 in the pot, and I'm left with just about $27,000 in chips.

—THE RIVER—

A break for me, I think. If he was on a draw, he missed. If he was calling me down with a queen hoping that I'd just keep bluffing my chips off, I just sucked out on him. If he happens to be holding a ten, I have a good chance of taking away all of his chips, unless he's managed to make a full house.

My options seem clear: Bet for value or check and hope to induce a bet. What would you do?

Checking—and hoping to induce a bluff—is certainly an option. But there are a number of medium-strength hands he could be holding that would make him happy to check behind me for a free showdown, hands like Q-J, K-Q, or Q-9. I think a value bet here is better. I just hope he's got enough of a hand to call me.

I bet $10,000. Marco hardly hesitates before raising me all-in. There is $73,600 in the pot, and it will cost me my last $16,200 to call.

Excuse me while I go throw up.

A fine mess I've gotten myself into. I have invested nearly two thirds of my chips into what has become a monster pot. The pot is offering me nearly 5–1 odds to call. I can fold and have $16,200 left, or I can call and pray.

What would you do?

It's in my best interest to call if there's even a small chance he might be bluffing. This hand is just too difficult to throw away. Marco might make this play with K-T, J-T, or T-9. I grit my teeth and push the rest of my chips into the middle.

Marco turns over J♠9♥, having flopped "the joint." I am bounced out of the tournament in twenty-seventh place.

I invested a lot of money in a hand I chose to play out of position, I ignored the danger signs as Marco smooth-called me from position, and I did more than my part to build a big pot with a hand that—at least until the river—fell far short of being a monster. Well done, Phil. Maybe next time I'll save myself some time and just hand Marco all of my chips.

❧ KEY ANALYSIS ❧

When a good player who respects your game just calls your bet after the flop, be very afraid—he or she is very often slowplaying a monster.

INSIDE MAN

THE SITUATION: Charity tournament supporting the Cancer Research and Prevention Foundation. There are eighteen players remaining, and an average stack of about $70,000.

——NO LIMIT HOLD'EM TOURNAMENT——
Blinds $1,000/$2,000

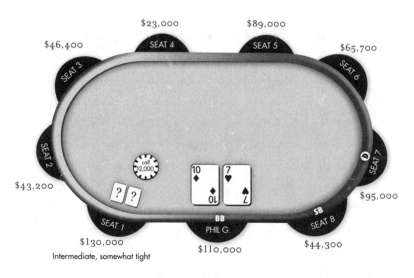

POT: $5,000   **TO CALL:** $0

A tight, fairly experienced player under the gun limps in. Everyone else folds, and the action is on me in the big blind. This doesn't happen every day. Technically speaking, I have two choices here—check and see the flop for free, or raise and hope to take the pot down right now.

What would you do?

The choice seems clear: Out of position, against the only player who can put me all-in, I'll rap the table and see the free flop.

——THE FLOP——

Hi-ya! I resist the overwhelming urge to karate chop the table, and I start thinking about what to do next. Check my straight and hope for some action, or bet out and hope for a raise?

What would you do?

While the desire to slowplay is strong, I think it's a mistake here. What kinds of hands is my opponent likely to be holding? A tight intermediate-skilled player who limps in under the gun generally has a very big hand—aces, kings, or possibly ace-king—and is hoping to re-raise a late position raiser. Or he has a hand like a middle pocket pair or a medium suited connector and is hoping to see a cheap flop. In either case I'm certain that I have the best hand and want to put him in position to make the biggest possible mistake: I want him to raise with an overpair or a set. Betting seems clear.

How much would you bet?

I want to make this painful for him if he really has limped with A-A or K-K. I rarely overbet the pot, but in this case I think it is justified. If he has the overpair, as I think and hope he does, I want it to be extraordinarily expensive for him to raise me.

I bet $8,000. My mark raises to $20,000. There is $33,000 in the pot, and it will cost me $12,000 to call.

Obviously I'll call . . . or re-raise. Before making my decision, I spend a little more time thinking about the kinds of hands he's likely to be holding here:

♦ A big overpair. This would be ideal. If he's got a hand like aces or kings, he's drawing nearly dead. This intermediate player will very likely overvalue his overpair.

♦ A medium pocket pair. Even if he's flopped a set, I'm still a 2–1 favorite to win. If he's flopped a set, he'll call or raise just about any bet I make.

♦ A flush draw. The only hand I would be an underdog to (albeit a very slight one) is J♣T♣, but it's not a hand he'd have been likely to limp in with from under the gun. A♣K♣ is a more realistic possibility, and would give him a nearly 40% chance of beating me with a flush.

In any case, I know three things:

1. I have the best hand right now.
2. I'm likely to have the best hand at the end.
3. I want to get all my chips in the pot, and get called, as soon as possible.

If I push all-in here, will he call me? Maybe, maybe not. What would you do? Call and trap on the turn, or raise? If you're going to raise, how much?

With all that flowing through my mind, I'm ready to act. I decide that I'm better off making a raise that he can call. I'll give him a chance to make another mistake on the turn.

I re-raise and make it $55,000. He glares at me for a minute before calling the bet. There is $115,000 in the pot.

—THE TURN—

9♠ 8♥ 6♠ K♠

While this might seem like a scary card for me, it's actually anything but: I am now sure he's not holding A♣K♣. If he's made a flush with some other cards, well, it's just not my day. I'm willing to go broke with my hand.

My options: Go for the check-raise or continue with a bet. What would you do?

I could try to get tricky with some kind of check-raise here, but there are two good reasons not to:

1. The pot has become huge.
2. My hand has become more vulnerable: If he's holding pocket kings or the A♣, he's just picked up a few more outs.

When the pot gets this big, I don't mind pushing all-in, as it gives me the best chance of protecting my hand against some weird suckout.

I push all-in. Seat 1 looks at me for a long time. "No way you'd play the hand like that with a flush draw on the flop. . . . You flop a set or something?"

I do my best to act like I've been struck by Medusa's gaze. After what seems like an hour, he slowly pushes his chips into the middle. "I call."

I turn over my straight. Seat 1's face seems to pinch into itself, like he's just eaten an entire lemon. "At least I have a few outs," he murmurs, flipping over A♣A♦.

"No clubs, dealer," I implore.

——THE RIVER——

We both flinch when the ace hits the river, as it takes me a second to remember that my straight beats his set.

"Tough beat," I say. Secretly I think he got exactly what he deserved. He limped in with aces and paid the ultimate price. He's obviously never heard the great T. J. Cloutier expound on pocket aces: "You either lose a big pot with 'em, or you win a small pot."

❧ KEY ANALYSIS ❧

Slowplaying has its moments, but you can often lure your opponent into making an even bigger mistake by betting and raising.

THE BUBBLE

THE SITUATION: Approaching the bubble of a $1,000 buy-in No Limit Hold'em tournament in Tunica, Mississippi. Twenty-seven players will make the money, and there are twenty-nine players left. Average stack is around $60,000.

——NO LIMIT HOLD'EM TOURNAMENT——
Blinds $1,000/$2,000 with $200 antes

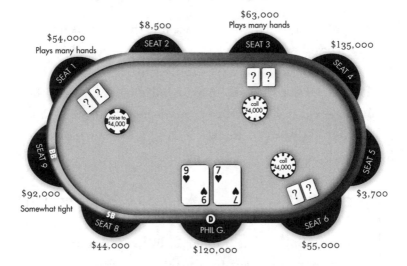

POT: $16,800   **TO CALL:** $4,000   **POT ODDS:** 4.2–1

A medium suited connector against a raise and two callers—an easy fold, right?

What would you do?

The chip-sandwich play—or as I like to call it, the fish-n-chips—becomes available any time a raiser (especially one with relatively loose raising requirements) gets called by one or more players (who probably would have re-raised with stronger hands). I re-raise and, if I can get that initial raiser to fold, I will usually wind up taking down a respectable pot without a confrontation. Oh yeah, it definitely helps that I have a commanding chip position.

There are a couple of other factors that help me here:

1. That commanding chip position I just mentioned. Even if I try this play, get called, and lose, I'll still have enough chips to put up a good fight.
2. We're near the bubble. A couple of the players at my table stand to get blinded off in the next round or two, not to mention the players at the two other remaining tables who might be in similar jeopardy. My opponents know this, of course, and will be less likely to risk all their chips when they can likely cakewalk their way into the money.
3. If I get called, I am not very likely to be dominated.

4. If I get called, I'll be in position and have control of the betting after the flop.

5. Neither the small blind nor the big blind are desperate yet. I definitely would not make this play if either of them were down to their last five to eight big blinds.

Yes, a careful analysis leads me to believe that this is a great time for Long John Silver's—I'm bringing out the old fish-n-chips sandwich. I raise to $16,000. Just as I announce the raise and slide some chips into the pot, the table next to us draws a huge crowd: It seems that three players are all-in!

Anticipating the imminently bursting bubble (and guaranteed payday), everyone folds quickly, and I scoop the pot.

Poker is an easy game, no?

❖ KEY ANALYSIS ❖

When you approach the bubble and notice a couple of players in danger of being blinded off, you can be pretty sure that your opponents have noticed the same thing! Many players will tighten up and wait it out. There should be plenty of opportunities to steal pots before the flop.

PUNKED!

THE SITUATION: Late in a multitable tournament at Bay 101. Just to be cute, they started all one hundred players with $100,000 in chips. Eighteen players remain on two tables. The average stack is about $600,000.

——NO LIMIT HOLD'EM TOURNAMENT——
Blinds $20,000/$40,000 with $5,000 antes

POT: $105,000   **TO CALL:** $40,000   **POT ODDS:** 2.6–1

During the early stages of a tournament, I like to play a very tight brand of poker. It's a strategy that pays double dividends: I avoid having to make difficult decisions with questionable hands, chasing after relatively small pots, and when I reach the middle rounds, where the antes kick in, I can exploit my tight image to commit cold-blooded larceny, stealing the blinds whenever I see a spot.

Thanks to the big blinds and antes, there is more than $100,000 in dead money waiting to be plucked from the middle of the table. With the final nine players getting paid, I sense that the table has tightened up a bit. When everyone folds to me on the button, I don't even need a particularly good hand to attempt a steal. Even if I get called, I'll still be getting nearly 2–1 odds on my investment, and the luxury of superior position. This Q-9 feels like a monster.

So I've given my strategy away: Clearly I'm going to raise. I see no reason to deviate from the standard, three times the big blind, so I make it $120,000. The Punk, a twenty-two-year-old Phil Hellmuth imitator—the ski jacket, sunglasses, and black baseball cap are all there— calls my raise from the big blind. I'm not all that unhappy about his call. There is $305,000 in the pot, I'm in position, I have exactly the right image, and I seriously doubt he wants to go broke this close to a tournament payday. Even ninth place in this tournament is serious beer money for a kid experiencing his first facial hair.

——THE FLOP——

Nice flop—top pair. The Punk checks to me.

What would you do?

Well, I'm not getting fancy. I raised before the flop, and I suspect that I have the best hand. With straight and flush draws abounding, a pot-size bet seems in order.

I bet $300,000. The Punk calls quickly, but I don't get a great read on the strength of his hand—must be the sunglasses and hat. There is $905,000 in the pot and I have a cool $900,000 left.

A quick call is occasionally a tell indicating that your opponent is on a draw. Regardless, I'm not too happy about the direction this is heading. With a small hand—and top pair with a mediocre kicker definitely qualifies as "small"—I want to do my best to play a small pot. This pot is starting to grow just large enough to make it difficult to let it go.

——THE TURN——

"I'm all-in," announces the Punk, pushing his chips into the middle with a flourish. He has me outchipped, so he can only (!) build the pot to $1,805,000. It will cost me my remaining $900,000 to call. I'm getting 2–1 on my money.

What would you do?

This situation has, in a word, *deteriorated*. Okay, Phil, think. What could he have?

His quick call on the flop seemed to say that he didn't have to think too much about his decision. Pocket eights or pocket fives? Most players would have raised with a set, given the flush draw on the board, but it's certainly possible. Maybe he called me with a suited ace (clubs, of course) and figures that even if he's not in front now, he has a chance to get there on the river. He might even have A-Q or A-8.

I have a suspicious feeling about this hand. If he was strong on the flop, why didn't he protect himself against a draw? And if he was on a draw, why did he call such a big bet on the flop?

If I were Phil Ivey, Phil Hellmuth, Phil Laak, hell, even Phil my barber, I might have the courage to call. Unfortunately, I'm just Phil Gordon, and I can't escape the voice in my head screaming, "Don't go broke with one pair!" Not just one pair, but second pair. With a crappy kicker. Am I really going to call here?

Calling and winning would feel great, but folding won't be so bad. I still have a near average stack and around twenty-three big blinds, enough ammunition to wait for a better spot. The only truly terrible outcome would be calling and losing.

What would you do?

"Nice hand, Devo," I say, tossing my cards into the muck.

"Who's Devo?" asks the Punk, grinning, and turning over 9♥5♦. Bottom pair! I would have been 95% to win! "Did I have you?" he asks, already knowing the answer.

"Sure did," I lie, pushing my lips together to make what I hope passes for a smile.

That hurt . . . but if I never get bluffed, then I know that I'm calling too much. I'm going to remember the play this kid made against me for a long time. With a little luck, we'll find ourselves back in this spot again soon.

KEY ANALYSIS

If I never get bluffed off a hand, then I am probably calling too much. Folding a dubious hand to maintain an average chip position in a tournament is rarely a "bad" play.

RUSHING TO DISASTER

THE SITUATION: Approaching the bubble of a tournament that pays twenty-seven places. Thirty-two players remain. The average stack is $50,000.

——NO LIMIT HOLD'EM TOURNAMENT——
Blinds $1,000/$2,000 with $300 antes

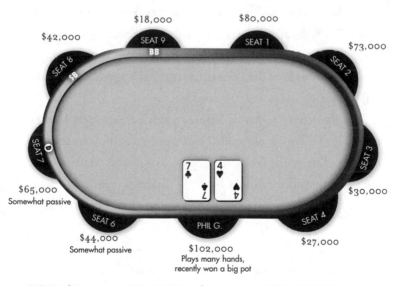

POT: $5,700   **TO CALL:** $2,000   **POT ODDS:** 2.9–1

I am a god of poker!

Or so it feels, the way I'm running over this table. I've got the big stack, and I've been getting great cards. I've shown down pocket aces *and* pocket kings in the last round alone. My raises are getting plenty of respect, especially now that we're approaching the bubble. I have nearly every "ante chip" on the table. These guys are letting me slap them silly. This is, in a word, fun.

I've just been dealt a terrible hand. . . . Is it worth going for a steal?

What would you do?

It doesn't really matter what I have here. I'm in the cutoff (okay, one seat to the right of the cutoff, but the way I'm running, who cares?), and I'm feeling the urge to steal. And why not? I decide to raise four times the size of the big blind, or $8,000.

Everyone folds to the big blind, who pushes all-in. There is $29,700 in the pot, and it will cost me $10,000 to call.

Okay, that sucks. In my excitement and euphoria I forgot one of my tournament mantras: Target the average stacks. The big blind, down to just nine big blinds, has chosen to take a stand. Can you blame him?

What would you do?

As sick as it sounds, the nearly 3–1 odds I'm getting from the pot almost force me to call him. If he's got an overpair to a seven, he's a huge favorite to win, but against any other hand, I'm not likely to be more than a 2–1 underdog. The money in the pot pretty much demands that I call.

I call the extra $10,000. The big blind turns over K♥9♠ and I'm about 35% to win. The community cards don't improve either of our hands, and he takes down the nearly $40,000 pot.

Yes, I made the mathematically correct play (after I'd been caught with my hand in the cookie jar, that is) but wound up investing nine big blinds to try to win a pot with 7-4 offsuit. An average-stacked player probably wouldn't have called with K-9, but a short-stacked player doesn't have the luxury of waiting for a premium hand.

I can think of a lot of ways to describe my play on this hand, and the words "winning poker" aren't on the list. I'm going to have a very difficult time getting any respect from the table after showing down that 7-4 offsuit. My image is ruined, I've lost 20% of my chips, and, worst of all, had I been paying closer attention to my opponents' stacks, it all could have been easily avoided.

❧ KEY ANALYSIS ❧

When you're out to steal blinds, target the average stacks. The big stacks can afford to call your bluff, and the short stacks don't have anything to lose. Realize also that turning over a truly terrible hand will do significant damage to your image and make the game much tougher to beat.

BIG HAND BIG POT, SMALL HAND SMALL POT, PART I

THE SITUATION: Late in the $500 buy-in, Friday afternoon tournament at Caesars Palace, Las Vegas. About thirty players remain, with twenty-seven spots paid. The average stack is about $100,000. My table has played relatively tight poker for the last half hour.

Blinds $2,000/$4,000 with $500 antes

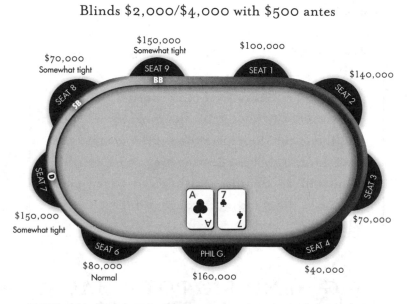

POT: $10,500   **TO CALL:** $4,000   **POT ODDS:** 2.6–1

Not that I'm superstitious (I think that's bad luck), but A-7 has been a lucky hand for me over the course of my career. With a well-above-average stack and a tight table, I might as well take a stab at stealing the blinds.

I raise to $12,000. The cutoff, the button, and the big blind all call. There is $54,500 in the pot. So much for stealing the blinds!

——THE FLOP——

Jackpot! The blind checks to me, and I've got two players to act behind me. Bet or slowplay?

What would you do?

I have flopped a very, very big hand. And when I flop a very, very big hand, I try to build a very, very big pot—especially in multiway pots.

Before I decide what to do, I consider what kinds of hands my opponents are likely to have called me with. Had they been dealt premium hands, most players would have been inclined to re-raise me before the flop. The fact that they just called suggests medium or low pocket pairs, hands like K-Q, Q-J, or A-9, and even suited connectors aren't outside the realm of possibility.

If someone has 8-7 or 7-6, I'm probably going to get a lot of action regardless of what I do next. I don't, however, want to make a big bet that will scare off a player with a hand like T-T, 9-9, or 8-8. Keeping in mind that I'm looking to build the biggest pot I possibly can, I want to try to trap some of their money in the middle. This is one of the rare situations where I'll slowplay and/or check-raise with a powerful hand.

I check. The cutoff bets $25,000. The button calls. The big blind folds. There is $104,500 in the pot, and it will cost me $25,000 to call.

What would you do?

You know that big pot I was hoping for? It just showed up. I could just call, in the hopes of luring even more money in on the turn, but I'll be out of position against my two remaining opponents. Will I check and hope they bet, or bet and hope they call? Do I really want to see an eight or a nine on the turn? Besides, have I mentioned that this is a big pot?

When the pot gets this large this late in a tournament, I don't think there's anything wrong with making an all-in move to take it down immediately. I may be sacrificing a little bit of equity later on down the line, but I'm not going to risk getting outdrawn.

I push all-in. The cutoff calls with his remaining $43,000; the button folds. The cutoff groans when I turn over my A-7. He flips over pocket nines.

"Give me a nine!" he yells at no one in particular. The turn is the 5♦, the river the 6♠. My big hand holds up to take a big pot.

> ## ❧ KEY ANALYSIS ❧
>
> When you flop a big hand, do what you have
> to do to create a big pot. When the pot gets
> big, don't be afraid to push all-in and take it
> down. These opportunities don't come around
> often, so when they do, you have to take full
> advantage.

BIG HAND BIG POT, SMALL HAND SMALL POT, PART II

THE SITUATION: Late in a tournament. About
thirty players remain; only twenty-seven will make
the money. The average stack is about $100,000. My
table has played relatively tight poker for the last hour
or so.

—NO LIMIT HOLD'EM—
Blinds $2,000/$4,000 with $500 antes

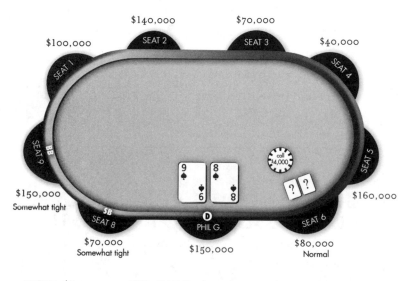

POT: $14,500   **TO CALL:** $4,000   **POT ODDS:** 3.6–1

I'm in position with a deep stack, have a decent hand that isn't likely to be dominated, and am receiving great odds from the pot. After Seat 6, the cutoff, limps in, I see no reason to get fancy—calling behind him seems perfectly acceptable.

I call the $4,000 bet. The small blind folds and the big blind checks. There is $18,500 in the pot.

——THE FLOP——

The big blind and the cutoff check to me. Do I bet my middle pair? How much should I bet?

Unless someone is slowplaying, my pair of nines might be the best hand right now. It's not likely to improve, and there's a potential straight brewing.

However, what I *don't* have is a big hand. Middle pair, weak kicker is by no means a powerhouse. And when I have a small hand, I do my best to play a small pot. I have to make a bet to protect my hand, but I don't want to start building a huge pot that I can't get away from. Betting about half the pot here sounds right to me.

I bet $9,000. The big blind calls and the cutoff folds. There is $36,500 in the pot.

——THE TURN——

The big blind checks to me. How much should I bet this time?

225

What would you do?

I'm not crazy about the fact that the big blind opted to call my bet on the flop. What could he have? A better question might be what he thinks that *I* have. Many aggressive players on the button will bet with almost anything when the betting gets checked around to them. From the big blind's view, I don't have to be holding any kind of legitimate hand to have thrown in my bet. He might have a medium pocket pair, or an ace with a decent kicker that he thinks might be good. He could also have a weak queen—something like Q-J or Q-T—or even a nine. I can't even discount the possibility that he has a four, in which case he's ecstatic over that turn card. His check to me might be a prelude to a big check-raise.

The point is, I don't really have a great sense of what he has. I've done a good job so far of keeping this pot small—there's less than half of an average stack in the middle—and throwing away middle pair would hardly be a catastrophe. Were I to make any kind of reasonable bet in this spot, I'd be charting a headlong course toward exactly the kind of meaningful pot I've been trying to avoid.

Winning poker has little to do with winning pots: Good money management plays a far more significant role. Yes, checking here may result in a free river card that might wind up costing me the pot. So be it.

I check. There is still $36,500 in the pot.

—THE RIVER—

The big blind checks.

This decision is even easier than the last. If I bet here, the only way I'm likely to earn a call is if I'm beaten. I'm unlikely to win any more money, and I certainly don't want to put myself in a position to lose any more than I've already invested. Betting medium-strength hands on the river is usually a very bad idea.

The big blind turns over J♥T♥ for a straight to the king. Looks like he was trying to trap me on the river.

Could I have driven him off with a big bet on the turn? Possibly. But he'd already shown his willingness (or maybe ignorance) to call with the worst of it on the flop. As it turned out, he had seventeen outs to beat me (any king, queen, jack, ten, or eight would have done the trick) and might have had a very hard time laying his hand down.

And I would have lost a big pot with a small hand.

✪ KEY ANALYSIS ✪

When you've got a small hand, do your best to play a small pot.

THE FINAL TABLE

For me final table poker is what the game is all about. To win the title all I have to do is outlast the few individuals sitting at the table. I can see them. I know how they play. I focus intensely and scrap for every chip. I use every trick in my playbook and exploit any edge, statistical or psychological, that I can find. The pressure is enormous, but so are the rewards.

It doesn't matter whether you're Phil Ivey or Phil the plumber from Cleveland—you have to get lucky to win a tournament. Many (if not most) of the pots I find myself playing will require life-and-death decisions. With a little luck, I've been able to build a big stack, allowing me both to put pressure on my opponents and to survive the inevitable hands where I'll get outdrawn. If I don't have a big stack, well, now's the time to get lucky!

Know this: When I play tournaments, I play to win. I am not playing to "move up in the money" and secure a slightly better payday. I'm looking for a win, the big *W*. I know my desire to win leads me to make an occasional play that might be incorrect from a strictly monetary perspective. I'm also pragmatic and know that the pay-out structure rewards you for winning. Outlasting 609 players at the 2001 *WSOP* to finish fourth earned me $399,610. Finishing second was more than a million, and Carlos Mortensen took home $1.5 million for first. Mathematics tells me to play to win—and the feel of that bracelet on your wrist isn't a bad reason either.

WHEN CRIME DOESN'T PAY

THE SITUATION: Final table of a $1,500 buy-in No Limit Hold'em tournament. Seven players remain.

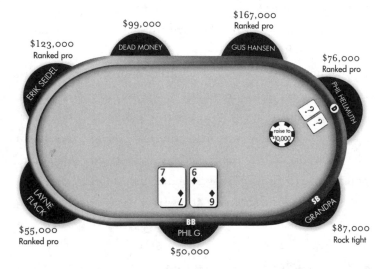

NO LIMIT HOLD'EM TOURNAMENT
Blinds $1,500/$3,000 with $500 antes

$99,000

$167,000
Ranked pro

$123,000
Ranked pro

DEAD MONEY

GUS HANSEN

$76,000
Ranked pro

ERIK SEIDEL

PHIL HELLMUTH

D

raise to $10,000

? ?

7♦ 6♦

LAYNE FLACK

$B GRANDPA

$55,000
Ranked pro

BB
PHIL G.

$87,000
Rock tight

$50,000

POT: $18,000   **TO CALL:** $7,000   **POT ODDS:** 2.6–1

Stealing the blinds to build a stack is a great tournament strategy when you can pull it off. At this table, however, that tactic is not working. The last three times I've tried, I've been re-raised by Layne and Erik. They just won't let me steal. I haven't been able to pick up a pot in what seems like hours, and my once-proud stack has been whittled down to about seventeen big blinds.

With the quality of the players at the table, I'm not feeling great about my chances.

And here I am facing yet another raise from Phil Hellmuth Jr., one of the best players in the world. You'd think I could catch a break.

I'm getting tremendous odds to call Phil's raise here—even if he's got pocket aces, I'm only about a 4–1 underdog. The downside is that I'll be playing a mediocre hand, out of position, against someone certainly capable of outplaying me on the flop. Oh yeah, and I'll have to risk nearly one seventh of my rapidly dwindling stack to see the flop.

What would you do?

I could fold, but at this point in the tournament if I'm going to compete against players this talented, I need some sort of viable strategy for gathering chips. Thanks to Erik's and Layne's relentless pressure, stealing the blinds from the button or cutoff is out. And no, waiting for aces or kings is not a viable strategy.

I have to give serious consideration to moving all-in against Hellmuth—a big "re-steal" attempt. Let's take a look at what can happen.

1. Hellmuth folds. Remember that he's the first to enter the pot and is raising from the button—an

obvious steal situation if ever there was one. Even if he has a reasonable hand, like K-Q or A-J, I still have enough chips to put a huge dent in his stack. If he loses, he'll only have $16,000 left. If I can take this pot without a showdown, I'll win about another six big blinds, adding around $17,000 (34%) to my stack.

2. Hellmuth calls. While it won't make me happy, things could be worse. Against A-K, I'm about 40% to win. Against a big pocket pair, I'm somewhere between 20% and 25% to win.

All things considered, I think it's worth the risk. Phil loves to raise from the button, and while he might not respect my game, I think he'll need an excellent hand to gamble with me here. There are players out there who don't mind "racing" with most or all of their stack, but Phil is not one of them. He's not under any pressure to do so here, as he can fold and still have about twenty big blinds.

"I'm all-in," I say, hoping my voice doesn't crack.

Phil stares at me through his Oakleys for what seems like an hour, but finally folds. "I'm going to snap you off if you keep that up," he snarls as he mucks his hand. I resist the temptation to show my piece-of-crap hand. As much as I'd like to tilt him, I might need that play again in a few rounds.

❖ KEY ANALYSIS ❖

When you can't steal the blinds, try re-stealing from the late-position preflop raisers. Even if they call, you're rarely in as terrible a shape as you might think. Aggression is the key to the game, and finding creative ways to be aggressive will win you pots you weren't supposed to win.

FISH-N-CHIPS

THE SITUATION: The final (televised) table at the 2004 Bay 101 Shooting Stars tournament. Six players remain.

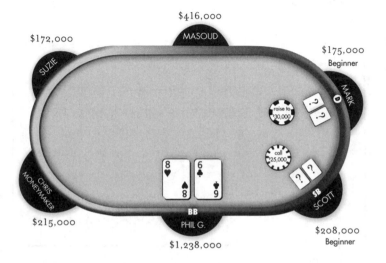

$416,000

$172,000

MASOUD

$175,000
Beginner

SUZIE

MARK

raise to
$30,000

call
$25,000

CHRIS
MONEYMAKER

8 ♥

6 ♠

8

9

SB

SCOTT

$215,000

BB
PHIL G.

$1,238,000

$208,000
Beginner

POT: $76,000   **TO CALL:** $20,000   **POT ODDS:** 3.8–1

The announcements are over, the players are seated. The crowd quiets as the first hand of the *WPT* final table is dealt. I have a massive, seemingly insurmountable chip lead. And, for once, I'm probably the best player at the final table, although world champion Chris Moneymaker might dispute that claim. I really think this should be a slam dunk; I have more than half of the chips in play. No player has ever come to the final table of a *WPT* event with a bigger percentage of the chips than I have now.

Mark, a Canadian businessman, raises to $30,000 on the button. Scott, one of Mark's best friends and an extremely rich young guy, calls from the small blind. It's $20,000 to me. I'm getting great odds on my money, and I've got plenty to spare.

What would you do?

In this situation, I'm getting tremendous odds even with a hand as crappy as 8-6 offsuit. Calling here would certainly be a decent option. I think that the better play, however, is to go for the chip-sandwich play:

♣ Neither player has demonstrated a lot of strength. Mark's raise from the button could very well be a steal attempt, and Scott probably would have re-raised him if he had a very strong hand.

♣ There is no one left to act behind me, that is, no chance of someone waking up with a monster hand.

♣ We've just started play at a televised table. No one wants to go home early when the TV cameras are running. This gives my play a better-than-normal chance of succeeding.

♣ Neither player is supershort-stacked. Both can fold without affecting their relative prospects of winning the tournament.

♣ I have a very big stack and have the ability to exert a lot of pressure on my opponents.

♣ If either of them call with a hand like A-K or A-Q, I won't be dominated. Against those hands I'll have about a 38–40% chance to win.

I'm the table captain, damn it. I raise to $240,000, enough to put both players all-in.

Mark folds quickly—usually a good sign that the fish-n-chips is going to work—but Scott seems to agonize over his next move. I just don't see how he can risk going broke here with what is obviously a less-than-stellar hand.

"All right, let's go. . . ." Scott pushes his remaining chips into the middle and calls. I'm not at all happy about it, but even if I lose the pot, I'll still have more than $1,000,000 in chips.

Scott turns over A♠J♥. I'm better off than I could have been. My 8-6 is only about a 1.7–1 underdog to his hand.

──THE FLOP──

The crowd gasps—the flop gives Scott top pair, but I have an open-ended straight draw. I get no help on the turn or the river, and Scott wins the $512,000 pot.

While it may look like I made a completely bone-headed play, consider this: I lost $238,000 chasing what turned out to be a $512,000 pot. In other words, thanks to the dead money in the pot, I was getting odds of about 1.2–1 to play. My decision to play Scott for all of his chips wouldn't have been too horrible even if we had both been playing with our cards faceup! I'd make the same play again today.

Though he decided to rip me in the telecast, Mike Sexton said to me later that day that he didn't think Scott would have called with A-J, and that he liked my aggressive play.

❖ KEY ANALYSIS ❖

The fish-n-chips play is an excellent weapon to have in your arsenal, especially when there is a lot of dead money on the table and you have the chip lead.

DRESSED TO THE NINES

THE SITUATION: The final table of a charity tournament. Three players remain.

——NO LIMIT HOLD'EM TOURNAMENT——
Blinds $15,000/$30,000 with $4,000 antes

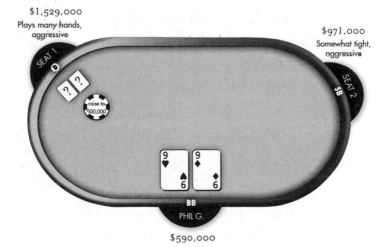

POT: $157,000   **TO CALL:** $70,000   **POT ODDS:** 2.2–1

Medium pocket pairs are among the most difficult hands to play in No Limit Hold'em, especially if you're out of position. Ideally, I'd find a way to see a cheap flop and hope to spike a third nine. As of this moment, however, I'm not living in that kind of world—it's going to cost me more than one-third of my stack to call this raise.

What would you do? Call and see the flop? Re-raise? Surely you wouldn't fold 9-9 in a three-handed game, right?

I don't *have* to get involved in this hand. I have nearly twenty big blinds, and while I'm hardly swimming in comfort, I'm at least a few orbits away from life support. Then again, if I start allowing Seat 1 to use his big stack to steamroll me, I'm going to be gasping for breath sooner than I'd like.

More important, I think I have the best hand. Sure, he could have aces. What's more likely, however, is that he's got *an* ace. Or two overcards. In a three-handed game, he doesn't need much of a hand to raise from the button.

When I have the best hand, I want to raise. But how much?

Say I re-raise to $300,000, adding another $270,000 to the pot. Seat 1 will be faced with calling another $200,000 to play for a $427,000 pot, creating pot odds (for him) of better than 2–1. With those odds, he'd be correct to call me with just about any hand that had an overcard to my nine. And with a big stack—and the chance to eliminate a pesky player—why wouldn't he?

If I raise more than $300,000, I'm going to have to risk more than half of my stack on this hand, which would leave me in awful shape in the unlikely event that I decide to fold after the flop. And how could I? I'll be more or less pot committed, and it would have to be an absolutely terrifying flop for me to even consider folding. Given the relatively small chances that I'll flop a set or better (11.8%) or see a board without an overcard (less than 10%), not to mention that I have an aggressive opponent who will certainly bet if I don't, I'm probably going to be faced with a very ugly decision after the flop, regardless of how I play this hand.

Since a big re-raise from me will probably force me to commit all my chips to the pot anyway, why not move all-in now? There are a couple of good reasons for doing so:

1. I probably have the best hand. If he's got a big pocket pair, I'm a 4.5–1 underdog, but against any other hand, I'm going to be favored to win an all-in showdown.
2. I still have "fold equity." A lot of fold equity, in fact.

An all-in bet from me leaves him with pot odds in the vicinity of 1.4–1. He's still mathematically correct to call me with two overcards (creating the proverbial coin flip), but he won't know that. And will he really want to risk doubling me up here? If he loses this all-in showdown to me, I will be the new chip leader. He's unlikely to call my all-in re-raise with anything short of A-J.

3. I will avoid having to make any difficult decisions after the flop. The chances of my losing my nerve in the face of a scary board will be reduced to zero.

"All-in," I say, moving my stack into the middle. It takes him about three seconds to fold, and I add a nice pot to my stack.

❧ KEY ANALYSIS ❧

Against an aggressive player looking to use a big stack to run over the blinds, the all-in re-raise with a short stack is a great equalizer.

PRELUDE TO A NIGHTMARE

THE SITUATION: The final table at the 2005 *WSOP* $1,000 No Limit Hold'em tournament. Eight players remain. We're all in the money, but first place wins a coveted *WSOP* bracelet and nearly $1,000,000.

──NO LIMIT HOLD'EM TOURNAMENT──
Blinds $4,000/$8,000 with $1,000 antes

POT: $48,000   **TO CALL:** $24,000   **POT ODDS:** 2–1

Let me check those again. Yep, still aces! Obviously I'm going to play them here. The trick is getting my opponent—David "the Dragon" Pham, one of the toughest players in the world—to lose a lot of chips to me. Do I call his bet, hoping to trick him into making a mistake later in the hand, or do I raise now and risk scaring him off?

Further complicating the situation: This scenario threatens to play out identically to a hand we played just a round ago. David raised from the cutoff, I re-raised from the small blind (with a hand much worse than aces!), and he decided to muck his hand.

What would you do?

When a player raises in front of my great hand, I go through a mental checklist before countering with a response.

♥ Am I in position? No. That's a good reason to re-raise here—I wouldn't mind taking the pot before the flop and negating my positional disadvantage.

♥ How good is my opponent? He's one of the best. Another reason to try to take the pot before the flop.

♥ How strong is his hand? Probably pretty strong. While he is in an obvious spot to steal the blinds, the fact that I played back at him the last time around makes it less likely that he'd attack me with a weak hand here. A re-raise from me now might encourage him to push all-in against me, a bet that I'd call, of course. I'd be a big favorite to double up and move into the chip lead.

♥ How does he like to play? Aggressively. It's tempting to let him slide into this pot and overcommit his chips after the flop. David's a great player, however, and tricking him into doing so won't be easy.

♥ How strong is my hand? There isn't one any stronger. There aren't too many flops that could get me to throw my hand away, which lends some support to the idea of simply flat-calling here and going for a trap.

♥ How many chips do I have? Less than he has. This is, in a weird way, good for me, as he's more likely to play back at me aggressively if he thinks that he can use his bigger stack to push me off my hand.

What would you do?

In the end, David's skill, my inferior position, and my short chip stack convince me to re-raise. I usually re-raise three to four times the amount that the initial raiser bet. In this situation I am going to opt for the lower end of the spectrum. I really want David to think that I'm "playing back at him" again, and that he can knock me off my hand with a big re-raise.

I re-raise to $73,000. He announces that he's all-in. I'm pretty sure my chips beat his into the pot. My mom, sitting in the audience, begins chewing her fingernails and craning her neck to get a better view of the flop. If I win this pot, I'll be the chip leader at the table and a favorite to win my first *World Series of Poker* bracelet.

He flips over T♣T♥, and is none too happy to see my aces. I am slightly better than a 4–1 favorite to win.

The flop is ten-free, but not so the turn. The dealer lays the T♦ on the table. My head starts to spin. My vision tunnels. I feel faint.

When the dealer burns and turns the river, I can't hear or see a thing except for the card itself—a worthless deuce. I'm out in eighth place. I shake my head, shake David's hand, and try to sneak away from the table without having to do an interview for ESPN.

To this day I have nightmares about that ten on the turn. I've been in a position to win a World Series bracelet five times in the last three years, but this is as close as I've ever come to being the chip leader at a table I could control with just a few players remaining. I take some solace from the fact that I played the hand correctly, but that doesn't help me get back to sleep when the nightmares come.

When a player raises in front of your great hand, be sure to consider all the factors that will help you to help your opponent make the biggest possible mistake. If you've recently employed the "re-steal," be aggressive and go for it again. More often than not, your opponent won't believe you. On the other hand, if you've been playing very tight, consider a slowplay.

FLYING BLIND

THE SITUATION: The final table at the 2004 Bay 101 Shooting Stars tournament. Six players remain.

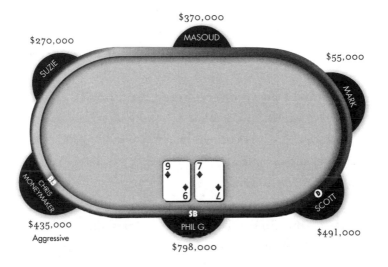

POT: $21,000   **TO CALL:** $5,000   **POT ODDS:** 4.2–1

What is there to say about the small blind? It's a horrible spot from which to play a hand. But late in a tournament, when the antes have kicked in and everyone folds around to you in the small blind, you're faced with the proverbial offer that you can't refuse. After all, with 4.2–1 odds, you'd be correct in taking 9-7 suited up against pocket aces!

I'm anything but immune to these kinds of offers. In fact, I probably play about 90% of the hands I'm dealt under these circumstances. I'm usually faced, however, with two competing goals: I want to win the pot, but I also want to lose as little money as possible if my opponent chooses to play back at me.

Should I play my hand here? If so, how?

What would you do?

Here's my breakdown for the small blind when everyone folds to me and I'm facing an "average" opponent (whatever that is).

- ♠ 75% of the time I'll raise three times the big blind, hoping to steal the pot without a confrontation.
- ♠ 10% of the time I'll fold.
- ♠ 10% of the time I'll limp in with a bad hand that I'll fold if the big blind raises.
- ♠ 5% of the time I'll limp in with a great hand that I'll re-raise with if the big blind raises.

Playing out of position against an aggressive player like Chris Moneymaker, I'd prefer to keep my investment to a minimum. I don't think Chris will "make a move" on me, considering my nice chip lead. If he does raise me, I'll give him credit for a good hand and I am likely to fold.

He doesn't raise but simply checks from the blind, and we see the flop with $26,000 in the pot.

——THE FLOP——

I wish I could say I had some kind of fail-safe secret for playing top pair, weak kicker from bad position, but we don't live in that kind of world. My first thought, as usual, is whether I should take the lead with a bet. There are several good reasons to do so here:

♦ There's a very good chance I have the best hand. Getting more money into the pot with the best hand is always a good idea.
♦ There are all kinds of possibilities for a straight to develop, and I don't want to give Chris a free chance to get there.
♦ While I think there's virtually no chance a bet will get Chris to fold a hand that is currently better than mine, I might get him to fold a hand that has a decent chance of catching up to me on the turn.

I want to bet enough to close out his draws. Somewhere between a half and two thirds of the pot should accomplish just that.

I bet $15,000. Chris raises to $45,000. There is $86,000 in the pot, and it will cost me $30,000 to call.

What would you do?

This is the pain of playing out of position. Because I didn't raise before the flop, I have absolutely no idea what two cards Chris is holding. He probably suspects that my hand is weak because I limped in from the small blind, and he is probably using his position (correctly) to push me out of this pot.

I know I should throw my hand away here. Chris, however, is capable of making some unorthodox plays. Before tossing my cards into the muck, I want to take a moment to think about what kinds of hands he might raise with:

♣ A better nine than mine. This includes overpairs to the board (although I'm nearly certain he would have raised from the big blind with a hand like that) as well as hands like 9-6, 9-4, and 6-4. All are possible, given the "free" look I gave him at the flop.

♣ A piece of the board. If Chris is holding a six or a

four, he has to consider the possibility that his hand is the best. A raise would give him a clearer picture and give him two ways to win: He could have the best hand or he could get me to fold. In position, it's nearly always right to "test" your opponent with a raise when the action develops the way that it has here.

♣ A draw. He's more than capable of semibluffing in this situation with a hand like 8-7 or 7-5, knowing that he has eight outs should I call his bet.

♣ Nothing at all. Chris knows that I am capable of bluffing at this pot. He also knows that since I gave him a free pass before the flop, I can't really narrow his range of starting hands. He can be representing any two cards, and unless I've flopped a set (unlikely, as I almost definitely would have raised with a pocket pair before the flop), I've got to fear a re-raise.

Truth be told, I don't have a very good idea where I stand. Maybe I should have raised before the flop after all. No time for regrets—I have to make a decision.

What would you do?

Should I re-raise? Probably not—I don't want to create a pot that I can't get away from with nothing to show but top pair, weak kicker. But I also don't think I can throw top pair away just because Chris has shown

251

moderate strength. When I don't have a strong feeling about raising or folding, I usually feel confident that checking or calling is the right play. It's only going to cost me another $30,000. . . . This is what a chip lead is for, isn't it?

I call his bet. There is $116,000 in the pot.

——THE TURN——

Well, I can't say I like that card. If he was playing 8-7, he just made his straight.

What would you do?

I check, another weak play, and wait to see what Chris does. I'm somewhat relieved to see Chris check behind me.

——THE RIVER——

The board is just getting nastier and nastier. The queen does nothing for my hand. But, given that Chris showed weakness on the turn by checking, is it worth making what will essentially be a bluff in the hopes of taking this pot?

What would you do?

At best I have a medium-strength hand, and I think that checking is the right play. If I bet, Chris will only call me with a hand that can beat me, and he'll fold every hand I can beat. In other words, a bet has no upside. If I check, Chris might check a hand that beats mine. He might also try to bluff the pot with a hand I can beat. Both of those possibilities are upsides. Checking is clearly the correct course of action.

Chris thinks for a minute, then bets $75,000. There is $191,000 in the pot, and it will cost me $75,000 to call.

What disaster have I gotten myself into this time? Chris checked behind me on the turn. . . . Was he slowplaying a straight, or did he feel like his hand was weak? Could the queen really have helped his hand? His relatively small bet is very strange. It seems like the $75,000 is begging for a call, but Chris might also be taking a weak stab at the pot with a busted straight draw or small pair. He knows that queen didn't make me happy.

Damned if I know. I do know that Chris's bet probably means one of two things:

1. He has a good hand (i.e., something better than a pair of nines). Good players don't like to bet medium-strength hands on the river.
2. He's bluffing.

So, $75,000 to look him up. What would you do?

I'm getting nearly 3–1 on my money, so if Chris would bluff here 25% of the time with a hand I can beat, I should call. In the end, that's exactly what I do, but I don't feel great about my decision.

I call his bet. Chris turns over Q♣9♥, for two pair, and happily drags in a $266,000 pot.

❖ KEY ANALYSIS ❖

It is extremely difficult to play hands from the small blind, as you're damned if you do (thanks to bad position) and damned if you don't (thanks to excellent pot odds.) When you're in the small blind, raising to give yourself a chance to win the pot before the flop is the best way to stay out of trouble. If and when you get called, play very carefully.

SUCKING OUT

THE SITUATION: The final table of a $200 buy-in tournament at FullTiltPoker.com. Four players remain.

——NO LIMIT HOLD'EM TOURNAMENT——
Blinds $3,000/$6,000 with $300 antes.

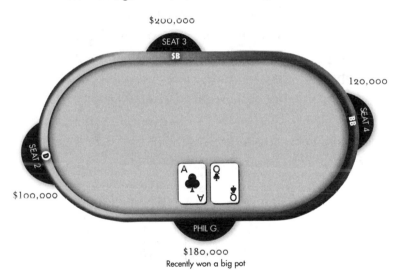

$200,000

SEAT 3
SB

120,000

SEAT 4
BB

SEAT 2
D

$100,000

PHIL G.

$180,000
Recently won a big pot

POT: $10,200   **TO CALL:** $6,000   **POT ODDS:** 1.7–1

During this last orbit I've run all over this table, taking the last three pots. No railbirds online? Now I've

255

got ace-queen suited, a fantastic starting hand in a four-handed game. I'm under the gun, second in chips, and ready for action.

What would you do?

Because I've played the last four hands, I think it is very likely that someone will try to "look me up" and play with me on this hand. With that in mind I'm going to make it expensive for them to do so: a raise of about four times the big blind seems right. Keep in mind that my bigger-than-normal raise doesn't have anything to do with the strength of my hand—I'm varying it because my opponents are less likely to respect a "normal" raise, given the number of hands I've recently played.

I raise to $24,000. The button calls—so much for position! The blinds both fold. There is $58,200 in the pot.

——THE FLOP——

No pair for me, but I have flopped a gut-shot straight draw with two overcards. I also have a runner-runner flush possibility. Do I make a continuation bet, check with the intention of raising, or check and consider folding to any action?

What would you do?

First I have to consider how likely it is that my opponent has connected with this flop. If he had a very strong hand, he probably would have re-raised my initial raise. If he had a very weak hand, he probably would have folded. My best guess is that he has a medium-strength hand. And many medium-strength hands have jacks and tens in them. I have to be very careful here.

Second, I need to think about his stack size. He has $76,000 left. If I bet any reasonable amount of money, even half the pot, and my opponent moves all-in, I will be forced to call his bet based on the pot odds. For example, say I bet $30,000 and he moves in on me. I'll have to call $45,000 to play for a pot of about $160,000. I will be getting nearly 4–1 pot odds to call, making my Break Even Percentage about 20%. I know I have four definite outs—any king will make me a straight—and the Rule of Four tells me I have a 16% chance of getting there by the river. Add in my runner-runner flush possibilities and the chance that I'll pair an overcard, and I will definitely be getting the right odds to call.

Do I really want to risk about half my remaining

stack on this hand? Not particularly. I decide to check. I'm really not sure what I'll do if he moves in on me, as many opponents might do in this spot.

My opponent checks as well, and I get to see a "free" turn card.

——THE TURN——

What a difference a card makes! I've gone from a man with limited prospects to the owner of a hand that gives me fifteen ways to win—nine flush outs, and six more non-clubs that will complete either end of a double gut-shot straight draw. Because he didn't bet the flop, I'm pretty sure that an ace or queen will win the pot as well. Just to be on the conservative side I'll only add three outs for those cards. That leaves me with an estimated eighteen outs.

I apply the Rule of Two and find that I have about a 36% chance of catching a winner on the river.

What would you do?

When a good turn card gives my hand a fighting chance to improve to a winner, I'll often think about semibluffing with a bet to try to take the pot. Here are some of the factors I consider:

♥ Did the turn give me additional outs? Yes, indeed!

♥ Has my opponent shown weakness? Yes—he simply called my preflop raise, and he failed to bet the flop when I checked to him.

♥ In my opponent's eyes, does it appear that the turn could have helped me? Possibly, if I had a hand like 8-8 or Q-9. I could also have been slowplaying a big hand on the flop in the hopes of trapping him with a check-raise.

♥ Is my opponent pot committed? Not yet.

♥ Will a semibluff commit me to the pot? Yes. If I make any reasonable bet, the pot odds will demand I call if he re-raises all-in.

♥ Can I bet enough to scare him off? Yes. I have him outchipped, we're in the money, and there is a significant difference in prize money between third and fourth place.

Betting seems to be the best option. With $58,200 in the pot and $76,000 remaining in his stack, I think I can exert maximum pressure by immediately moving him all-in. I'd prefer to take the pot without a showdown, but with all of the outs I have, I won't mind too much if he calls.

I go all in. He calls me without hesitation, flipping his A♠J♠ onto the table. A strong hand—he has top pair—but I have eighteen outs. Any club, any nine, any king, or any queen will win the hand for me. I'm taking the worst of it from an equity perspective, but only slightly so.

The river is the 9♥, completing my straight. I bust him, take the chip lead, and then have to suffer through a barrage of observer chat:

> Online Poker is Fixed!
> Rigged!
> What a suckout!
> RRIIIIIIIGGGGGEEED!
> Phil, big fan, can I ask you a question?
> Do you have a little "river me" button over there, Phil?

As the dust begins to settle, it's clear that both of us were almost destined to get all of our money into the pot on this hand—A-Q and A-J suited are huge hands in a four-handed game. Yes, I had to catch a card on the river; then again, he got lucky to flop top pair against a hand that had him dominated before the flop. I didn't get lucky to win the pot: I got lucky the moment I was dealt A-Q versus A-J in a four-handed tournament situation against the short stack.

And, no, online poker is not rigged, and I don't have a "River Me" button.

❈ KEY ANALYSIS ❈

When the turn card increases the number of outs you have against a player who has shown weakness, semibluffing becomes a potent option. With a semibluff you have two ways to win: You can either get your opponent to fold, or you can draw out (or, in this case, suck out) and make the best hand.

I FOUGHT THE LAW

THE SITUATION: The final table at the 2005 *WSOP* $1,000 No Limit Hold'em tournament. Nine players remain.

—NO LIMIT HOLD'EM TOURNAMENT—
Blinds $4,000/$8,000 with $1,000 antes

$225,000 — PASCAL PERRAULT

$550,000 — CHUCK THOMPSON

$135,000 — SHANE SCHLEGER BB

$70,000 — MENG LA

$175,000 — MICHAEL GRACZ SB

$300,000 — DAVID PHAM

$520,000 / Plays many hands — C.T. LAW D

$120,000 / Somewhat tight — PHIL G.

$250,000 — SHAE DROBUSHEVICH

POT: $21,000   **TO CALL**: $8,000   **POT ODDS**: 2.6–1

Things are starting to look bleak. I'm down to fifteen big blinds, second-to-last in chips. I remind myself that I'm not looking to move up in the prize money but that I'm playing to win, and K-Q in the cutoff seems like a pretty good place to start after everyone folds to me. I'm going to play this hand. . . . Should I make a standard raise or push all-in?

What would you do?

262

If I had only eight or ten big blinds left, I'd move all-in without a second thought. In this case, however, I have a little wiggle room. I've been playing very tight, and a "regular" raise here should garner enough respect to give me a chance at stealing the blinds. Fifteen big blinds is just too much to risk on a pot this small with three players left to act behind me—I think the conservative approach is best.

I raise the pot and make it $28,000 to go. C. T. Law—a decent, if somewhat loose, player with a huge stack—decides to call from the button. The blinds fold and hope for carnage. Eliminating me moves everyone up the prize ladder, and I know that Shane, in particular, could use the extra money after I whooped his ass earlier playing Roshambo in front of ESPN's cameras.

There is $77,000 in the pot.

——THE FLOP——

This is a terrible flop for me: no pair and no real draw. The only bright spot is that it probably wasn't a very good flop for C.T., either. Do I bluff at this pot or check and see what happens next?

Tough decision. What would you do?

I only have $92,000 left to fight for $77,000 in the pot. Even if I bluff here with all of my chips, C.T. would be "priced in" with just about any reasonable hand or draw. Checking and folding seems to be the more prudent option. I'll still have more than ten big blinds and will get to see seven hands before the blinds reach me again. I think I can find a better spot to risk my tournament life. I check, mentally committed to folding to any action. Fortunately, C.T. fails to exploit his position and big stack, opting to check behind me. I get to see the turn card for free.

——THE TURN——

Bingo! A great card for me. I'm almost certain that my pair of kings is currently the best hand. A bet will probably win the pot for me. Another possibility: I could check and hope to induce a bet from C.T.

What would you do?

When my hand improves on the turn, I look for a way to get my opponent to make the biggest mistake possible. While I'm obviously willing to risk all of my chips in this situation, I think my best play is to make a weak bet at the pot, one that looks and smells like a desperate steal attempt. I bet $28,000, about one third of the $77,000 pot. I have $64,000 remaining.

C.T. thinks for about twenty seconds, then raises to $56,000, just doubling my bet. There is $161,000 in the pot, and it will cost me another $28,000 to call.

An intriguing response from C.T. As I said earlier, there's no way I'm going to fold this hand in this spot. If he has me beat, more power (not to mention all of my chips) to him. That leaves me with two options: Call his mini-raise (and try to trap the rest of his money on the river) or move all-in now.

What would you do?

I think my choice is 100% clear: all-in, baby! With such a big stack, there is little chance that C.T. will fold to my bet unless he was on a stone-cold bluff. If he is bluffing, I'm not going to get any more money from him by just calling here and betting the river.

"All-in," I say. C.T. calls, then groans when I turn over my K-Q. . . . He has K♠T♠, and I've got him dominated. As long as I can avoid a ten on the river, that is. . . .

The river is the 4♦. I am back in business, and, for the first time in the last twenty hours of play, I have an above-average stack. C.T. missed two opportunities to take this pot away from me—a preflop re-raise or a bet on the flop would have sent me running for cover. His weak play cost him. It's also worth noting that my conservative play before the flop worked to my advantage—had I decided to push all-in with my fifteen big blinds, C.T. almost certainly would have folded his hand. I would have won only the blinds and antes, and my chip situation would have been a lot more desperate than it is now.

❖ KEY ANALYSIS ❖

With fifteen big blinds late in a tournament, don't be in a hurry to go all-in before the flop. You still have some room to maneuver. And when your hand improves on the turn, look for ways to make your opponent make the biggest possible mistake.

THE OPPOSITE

THE SITUATION: The 2003 Ultimate Poker Classic. Four players remain.

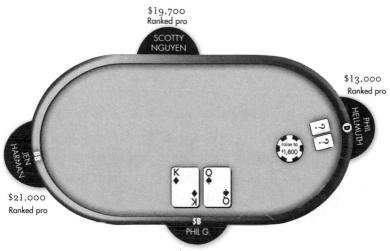

—NO LIMIT HOLD'EM TOURNAMENT—
Blinds $300/$600 with $75 antes

$19,700
Ranked pro

SCOTTY
NGUYEN

$13,000
Ranked pro

PHIL HELLMUTH

raise to $1,800

JEN HARMAN

$21,000
Ranked pro

$SB
PHIL G.

$30,000

POT: $3,000   **TO CALL:** $1,500   **POT ODDS:** 2–1

Ever see the episode of *Seinfeld* called "The Opposite"? It dawns on George Costanza that there's a simple explanation for his (many) failures in life: Every instinct he's had, every decision he's made, has been wrong.

"If every instinct you have is wrong," muses his friend Jerry, "then the opposite would have to be right."

Throughout my poker career I've always tried to

make the "right" plays. If you play in a straightforward style all the time, however, an expert player will pick apart your bankroll. Against an opponent who knows your game better than you do, mixing up your game is the only way to succeed.

Phil Hellmuth Jr. is one of those opponents. When it comes to reading a player's actions and putting people on a hand, Phil may have equals, but nobody's better. Not surprisingly, it's very, very difficult to outplay Phil at the table. To paraphrase one of the most important aspects of David Sklansky's Fundamental Theorem of Poker: You win money at the poker table when your opponents don't do what they should, or what they *would*, do if they could see all of your cards. Phil is usually so good at using your actions to guess your cards that you might as well be playing with your hole cards exposed.

How do you beat an opponent like this? Well, if he can guess everything that I'm going to do before I do it, then every instinct I have must be wrong. And if every instinct I have is wrong, then the *opposite* must be right.

Take this hand we played a few years ago at the Ultimate Poker Classic in Aruba. . . . Phil's preflop raise looks like a textbook attempt to steal the blinds. My K-Q isn't a powerhouse, but it's a very good hand, and may very well be better than whatever Phil happens to be holding. Given my big chip lead—and the fact that I'll be out of position throughout the hand against one of the best players in the world—my first instinct is to re-raise and try to win the pot before the flop.

What would you do?

Well, in this case, doing the opposite might just confuse Phil enough to cause him to make a big mistake. He'd expect me to re-raise with this hand, as I've done against him every time we've faced off over the last few years. This time I'm just going to call.

There is $4,500 in the pot.

——THE FLOP——

Ding! Top two pair, and a great chance to bust Phil Hellmuth on television. What could be better?

What would you do next?

My normal action in this situation, when there are plenty of potential straights and a flush draw on the board, is to bet. Great . . . except that I'm doing the opposite. I check, praying that Phil will bet.

Hellmuth checks behind me. There is still $4,500 in the pot.

——THE TURN——

I'm starting to like this opposite strategy. I gave him a free card, and now I've made a full house! What would you do now? Bet right out, or check and hope Phil hangs himself?

Normally, after Hellmuth had shown weakness by checking the flop, I'd check and hope he bets here, or even takes another free card that gives him something worth betting with on the river. Time to do the opposite—I'm going to bet. With $4,500 in the pot, I want to give Phil the right odds to chase a flush or straight draw—a draw that will leave him broke.

I bet $1,200, a small enough bet for him to continue with a drawing hand. To my delight, Phil calls defiantly, staring me down. Stare at me all you want, Mr. World Champion—I've got the nuts. And thanks to my opposite strategy, I'm pretty sure he doesn't have a clue as to what I'm holding.

There is $6,900 in the pot, and Phil has $10,000 left.

——THE RIVER——

Unfortunately, that river card isn't likely to have helped him. My normal strategy in this spot is to do my best to figure out what the "maximum extraction" number is—the most money my opponent might be willing to call—and bet that amount. Phil's call on the turn tells me either that he was on a draw (that just missed) or that he's got a hand strong enough to call another decent-size bet. After all, he knows that the 4♣ wasn't likely to have helped my hand, either.

Except that I'm doing the opposite. What would it look like if, instead of making a small, "callable" bet, I massively overbet the pot? Since Phil only has $10,000 left, it might look like I am trying to bully him with my bigger stack and a missed draw. I certainly wouldn't make a bet that big if I wanted him to call my flush or full house, right?

Wrong! I'm doing the opposite! I make a large, nearly pot-size bet of $6,000. Phil looks utterly confused. He should be! I haven't made a single "normal" play this entire hand.

Phil stares daggers at me. Finally, looking a little sick to his stomach (how nice that someone else is finally experiencing a bellyache), he decides to call.

I pull out a hand ranking chart I'd been holding in my pocket for such an occasion and pretend to have forgotten just how powerful full houses are. Some observers are amused when I slow-roll my queens full of kings. Phil is not among them. I go on to win this, the professional division of the tournament, only to get crushed by the "amateur" I face in the finale.

This tournament was part of the inaugural season of the *World Poker Tour*, and in the years since Phil and I played this hand, I've had a chance to see it several times on TV. There are two aspects to the outcome that continue to amaze me:

1. I can't believe what a jackass I was to slow-roll that hand. Phil actually showed quite a bit of restraint on and off camera after that incident. I have since apologized to him for my Hellmuth-like behavior.
2. I can't believe Phil didn't lose all his chips to me!

As it turned out, he was holding Q-6. He turned trips and not only didn't go broke but lost the bare minimum. If I had improved to trips on the turn with a short stack in front of me, all of my chips would have raced to the middle. Despite my "opposite" strategy, Phil's incredible instincts still found a way to ensure his survival.

❖ KEY ANALYSIS ❖

Playing "correct" poker all the time will make you predictable. Mix up your play to keep your more skilled opponents guessing and confused. Sometimes the right play is the wrong play, and vice versa.

SITUATION: CRITICAL

THE SITUATION: A really big online tournament, $200 buy-in, at FullTiltPoker.com. The first prize money is $20,000 . . . not a bad return on a $200 investment!

$155,000

$130,000

MAX
CORKLE

JANICKI
D

raise to
$12,000

? ?

TORMENTAS

SB

TOMMYGUN

$83,900

7♠

2♦

BB
PHIL G.

$240,000
Recently won a big pot

$8,000
Recently lost a big pot

POT: $18,500   **TO CALL:** $8,000   **POT ODDS:** 2.3–1

If I close my eyes, I can almost hear the sounds
of an electrocardiogram—I am on life support, and my
chances of survival don't look good. One hand earlier
I got all my money in before the flop with A-K, only to
suffer a terrible beat when TommyGun sucked out with
his dominated A-6. I know people say poker isn't a sport,
but I feel like I've been kicked in the stomach. After post-

ing my blind I have only $8,000 remaining . . . just two big blinds.

The first three players fold, and I allow myself the brief fantasy that I'll win this pot without a showdown. TommyGun pulls me back to reality with a raise big enough to put me all-in, of course. What a great time to have 7-2 offsuit, the worst hand in poker.

What would you do?

Well, since crying isn't an option, I suppose I'm going to have to make the right play, whatever that turns out to be. I'm getting pot odds of 2.3–1 to call, giving me a Break Even Percentage of 1 ÷ 3.3, or about 30%. The question I have to ask myself is this: Will 7-2 offsuit win 30% of the time?

Fortunately, I've done a lot of work with poker simulators, allowing me to answer questions just like this almost automatically.* Against a random hand—and let's face it, TommyGun could be attacking me with any two cards—my 7-2 offsuit has about a 35% chance of winning. I hate this hand, but calling is the right play.

I call. TommyGun shows J-5 offsuit. I fail to improve and get bounced from the tournament.

---

* If you haven't done so, spend some time experimenting with a poker simulator that allows you to see how certain hands do against others. One of the best on the market is produced by Donohoe Digital and is available at www.ddpoker.com.

When you have an extremely short stack in the big blind, it is usually correct to call the rest of your chips with any two cards. Even the worst hand in Hold'em is only a 2–1 underdog against a random hand.

POSITIONAL PARADISE

THE SITUATION: The final (televised) table at the 2004 Bay 101 Shooting Stars tournament. Five players remain.

—NO LIMIT HOLD'EM TOURNAMENT—
Blinds $8,000/$16,000 with $2,000 antes

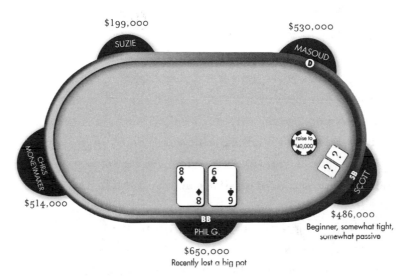

$199,000 — SUZIE

$530,000 — MASOUD (D)

raise to 40,000

? ? (SCOTT, SB)

$486,000
Beginner, somewhat tight,
somewhat passive

CHRIS MONEYMAKER — $514,000

BB — PHIL G.
$650,000
Recently lost a big pot

POT: $66,000 **TO CALL:** $24,000 **POT ODDS:** 2.8–1

After beginning this day with a huge chip lead—and huge hopes—I quickly fall into a downward spiral that has cut my stack in half. I seem to be losing hand after hand, my raises are getting no respect, and my once-commanding lead has been whittled to just a slim margin. I've been forced to switch gears, playing very tight poker for the last three orbits. So tight, in fact, that I haven't been involved in a single pot. I sincerely hope my opponents have noticed.

When everyone folds to Scott in the big blind, he raises to $40,000. Good pot odds, bad hand.

What would you do?

Why in the world would I consider calling a raise in this situation? There are actually a lot of good reasons:

♠ I need some chips.

♠ I have position.

♠ My hand isn't easily dominated.

♠ I've rebuilt my "tight" image, or so I hope.

♠ Scott plays a tight-passive game, and will be very scared to invest chips after the flop.

♠ Contesting the pot will make Scott think twice about trying to steal my blinds in the future.

♠ If this play works, I'll look like a genius on TV!

I call the additional $24,000. There is $90,000 in the pot.

——THE FLOP——

At least I flopped a pair. . . . The bad news is that the queen and jack are both cards that could easily have given Scott a better pair.

He fires a $30,000 bet into the pot, bringing the total to $120,000 and giving me 4–1 odds on the call.

What would you do?

My instinct for self-preservation makes me gulp and think about folding. This is why my "script" is so important—by forcing myself to consider raising before any other option, I'll often be rewarded with a clearer picture of the events in front of me.

Scott's bet was small. Very small. Smaller, in fact, than his preflop raise. While the board texture isn't terrifying, there are straight possibilities out there. . . . Shouldn't he be more afraid of them? I'm left thinking one of three things is happening:

♦ He's not afraid of the straight possibilities because *he* has a straight draw.
♦ He's not *just* afraid of the straight draw. The flop hasn't done much to help his hand, and he doesn't want to risk too much money on a continuation bet.
♦ He has a monster hand—a set, maybe—and he's trying to lure me into making a move.

If either of the first two theories is true, my correct action is to raise. If he's on a straight draw or missed the flop, my pair of sixes stands to be good right now, and I want to charge him to see the turn card. Even if my sixes aren't good, a raise might get him to throw away a hand like 9-9, A-J, or A-K. If I raise and he happens to have a monster hand, he's probably going to come over the top and go all-in—a bet I obviously have no intention of calling.

Summoning some courage, I raise to $90,000.

Scott ponders his decision for almost a full minute before calling. There is $270,000 in the pot.

Interesting . . . was he calculating pot odds, or just trying to get a read on me? His call gives me the impression that he has a hand like A-K or A-T—both gut-shot straight draws with some potential to pair an overcard. I hope my radar is working properly.

——THE TURN——

A great card for me! It's nearly impossible that it has helped Scott. If my sixes were good before, they're still good now. Scott seems to consider betting out, then, after a moment, checks to me.

What would you do?

Scott's "fake bet" is a classic tell. By acting like he's

got a hand that he has to consider betting with, he hopes to convince me not to bet behind him. I'm now nearly certain that even if my hand isn't the best, I've got a chance of winning this pot with a bet.

With $270,000 in the middle, this is no longer a tiny pot, especially when you remember that the average stack among the remaining players is only about $475,000. At this point in the tournament, any pot containing more than half of the average stack is worth attacking with a big move. My hand isn't likely to improve, and there are plenty of cards on the river that will kill my hand.

I'm not afraid to overbet the pot here. Scott has shown weakness the last two times he's been confronted with a decision. He obviously doesn't want to lose all of his chips on this hand. Mike Sexton may ridicule me on the TV broadcast, but I'm going to back my read with action: I bet $235,000.

Scott looks like he wants to puke. I know the feeling, buddy. He toys with his cards for a couple of minutes before tossing them into the muck.

Later I'll learn that Scott was holding A-K. His small bet on the flop was actually a sneakily good play, as he was giving himself the correct odds to chase the ace, king, or ten that would have given him a winning hand. His laydown on the turn, while painful, was also the right thing to do. His downfall was giving up control of the betting and playing out of position.

❖ KEY ANALYSIS ❖

Many players become tight and/or passive during the late stages in a tournament. You can often exploit these traits by playing more loosely and more aggressively. Trust your reads and have the courage to make a big play when the time is right.

BUYING AMMO

THE SITUATION: The final table at the 2001 *World Series of Poker* championship. Seven players remain.

Blinds $10,000/$20,000 with $3,000 antes

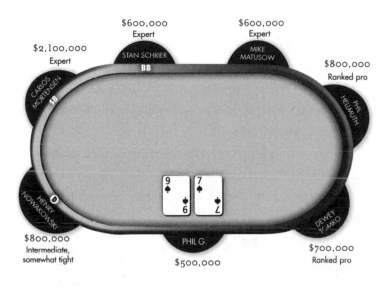

POT: $51,000   **TO CALL:** $20,000   **POT ODDS:** 2.6–1

The 2001 *World Series of Poker* championship final table is chock-full of talented players. Next to conservative amateur Henry Nowakowski, I am probably the weakest player remaining. I'm also on the short stack. "Phil," I say to myself, "hang in there. You're just two double ups from the chip lead. All you have to do is make quality decisions."

The more pressing issue is what to do with this 9-7 suited I've been dealt in the cutoff . . . raise and try to steal the blinds, or fold and wait it out.

What would you do?

At this point in the tournament every round of blinds is substantial. If I'm going down, I'm going down swinging. If I make a mistake, it's going to be an aggressive mistake. All tight play is going to get me is trampled by the pros who surround me.

I raise to $65,000. Henry, with little hesitation, re-raises to $140,000. Everyone else folds. There is $256,000 in the pot, and it will cost me another $75,000 to continue against Henry.

What would you do?

I am clearly not happy about this development. . . . Henry has position and the bigger stack, and his small raise smells fishily like a premium hand. The pot odds, however, are great for me—I'm getting better than 3–1 to call—and if there's a weaker spot than me at the table, it has to be Henry. If I'm going to have a chance of beating the likes of Hellmuth, Matusow, Tomko, and Mortensen, I'm going to need some ammunition. I'm going to feel silly if I go broke to Henry, but I don't see any easier paths to improving my stack than to meet him head-on.

I decide to call and pray for a big flop that can get

me back in contention for the title. The pot is up to
$331,000, and I have $360,000 left.

——THE FLOP——

Hallelujah! Talk about an answer to my prayers.
Top two pair! I look calm on the outside (or so I hope),
but on the inside I'm simultaneously doing a spit-take,
rubbing the astonishment out of my eyes, and perform-
ing a set of very awkward-looking jumping jacks. Now,
back to business. How do I play this hand? Bet right out,
or go for a check-raise?

What would you do?

As I've already noted, Henry is a conservative player.
He either has an overpair or a hand like A-K or A-Q. If
he has an overpair, it really doesn't matter how I play the
hand—he's going to put all of his money into this pot. If
he has A-K or A-Q, he's not going to call a bet, but he
just might bet if I check to him. Even if he checks behind
me, I'm not at all afraid of giving him a free card: He's
very unlikely to catch up.

While I'm not normally a huge fan of check-raising,
I think this is a pretty good spot to go for it. I'm short-

stacked, which encourages him to play aggressively against me, he has control of the betting due to his preflop raise and position, and I'm not afraid of giving him a free card.

I check to Henry. He considers the board and then bets $100,000. Nice! There is $431,000 in the pot now and I still have $360,000.

What would you do?

It's time to drop the hammer and move all-in. If Henry has an overpair, he'll definitely call, and the pot's grown big enough for him to consider calling with A-K or A-Q as well.

I move all-in. I hear my mom, seated in the audience next to my sister, gasp. The rest of the crowd stands on its feet. So does Mike Matusow, who, despite not being in the hand, paces nervously around the table.

Henry is faced with investing an additional $260,000 to win $791,000, nearly 3–1 odds. He is taking a very long time to decide, so I suspect he's on A-K. If so, and he puts me on a hand like T-T, J-J, or Q-Q, he'll think he's getting the right pot odds to call.

I'm getting close to peeing in my pants, when Henry finally rises and says, in his gentlemanly Dutch accent, "Okay, Phil, let's do it."

He turns over A-K, and my two pair hold up to win. I double up and am back in contention. Henry, crippled by the loss, goes broke to Phil Hellmuth two hands later.

❖ KEY ANALYSIS ❖

When you're at a tough table, sometimes it pays to take extra risks against the "easy" players. You'll need the ammunition to confront the better ones. When you hit a big hand, take a minute to figure out the right way to play it: Put your opponents on a likely range of starting hands and figure out how to get them to lose the most money to you.

WAR GAMES

THE SITUATION: The final table of a $500 buy-in tournament at the Horseshoe in Tunica, Mississippi. Six players remain.

──NO LIMIT HOLD'EM TOURNAMENT──
Blinds $500/$1000 with $100 antes

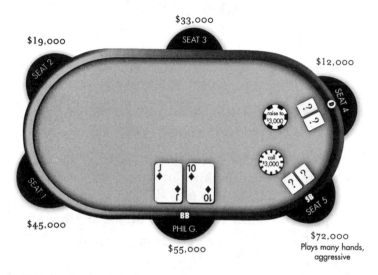

POT: $7,600   **TO CALL:** $2,000   **POT ODDS:** 3.8–1

I don't like to play too many hands out of the blinds, let alone call raises with them, but this jack-ten suited is a good, tricky hand that can really hit the flop hard.

What would you do? Call the raise or chuck it in the muck?

Come on, admit it. You'd call and be very happy about it. I sure am too.

There is $9,600 in the pot.

——THE FLOP——

Hi-ya! Top pair with a flush draw and a backdoor straight draw! Even if I don't have the best hand right now, I have a lot of ways to improve my hand: Three outs to two pair, two outs to trips, and another nine outs to the flush. Using the Rule of Four, I'm about 56% likely to improve my hand by the river, and that's not including a percentage point or two for catching running cards to a straight.

The small blind checks to me. Do I bet a lot and try to take the pot now? Bet a little to keep them on the line? Or check and wait for one of my outs before investing any more money into the pot?

What would you do?

Because the preflop aggressor is so short-stacked, I'm very confident that he'll take a shot at the pot if I check to him. It's a bet I'm happy to call: Even against pocket aces or kings, I'm a favorite to win. And it's no big deal if he checks behind me; he'll just be giving me a free shot at catching one of the fourteen cards in the deck that will improve my hand.

I check. The short stack pushes all-in with his last

$9,000, and I'm feeling euphoric—until the small blind calls *immediately*. There is $27,600 in the pot, and it's going to cost me $9,000 to call.

What could the small blind have? He didn't re-raise before the flop, so he probably doesn't have a huge hand. Nor did he lead out with a bet to protect his hand on the flop. And now he's decided to just call the button's all-in bet, leaving me with pretty good pot odds (3–1) to call into a board rife with flush and straight possibilities.

A set or top two pair seem unlikely—he'd probably only check with those hands if he intended to check-raise, and he's missed his opportunity to do so. With top pair and a better kicker than mine, he would likely have led out with a bet on the flop. My best guess is that he's on some kind of draw himself, or he's trying to keep the short stack "honest" by calling with a weak- or medium-strength hand, like middle pair.

What would you do?

No matter what he has, I benefit by raising. If he's on a draw, I'll be killing his odds. If he's got a weak- or medium-strength hand, I'll be applying a lot of pressure on him to fold. Secure in the theory that my hand is more than 50% likely to improve, I don't mind exerting the maximum amount of pressure available to me.

I raise all-in, giving myself two ways to beat the

small blind—he can fold, or I can draw to the best hand.

The small blind looks at me as though I've just stolen his cat. He appears to be thinking about calling, until his hands, seemingly detached from the rest of his body, toss his cards into the muck.

I turn over my J♦T♦. The button shows (gulp!) A♦8♦. All of those flush cards I thought I had working for me have suddenly become potential daggers to the heart. That said, my pair is the best hand right now, and I have about a 60% chance of still being in the lead after the river card.

The turn is the 5♣, and the river is the K♠, eliciting a loud, plaintive wail from the small blind, who claims to have thrown away K-Q. My pair of tens holds up to take the pot, and I'm one step closer to winning this tournament.

❦ K E Y A N A L Y S I S ❦

If you have a greater than 50% chance of improving your hand after the flop, don't be afraid to play your hand ultra-aggressively: It's a hand to bring to war. By exerting pressure on your opponents, you give yourself two ways to win: They can fold or you can draw to a winner.

IT'S ALL OVER, BABY!

THE SITUATION: The 2003 Ultimate Poker Classic. Three players remain, two of whom are drinking piña coladas. (The third is guzzling beers.) Scotty Nguyen (the beer drinker) has just survived an all-in confrontation with 5-4 suited to double up and is feeling very, very good about his chances.

——NO LIMIT HOLD'EM TOURNAMENT——
Blinds $1,000/$2,000 with $300 antes

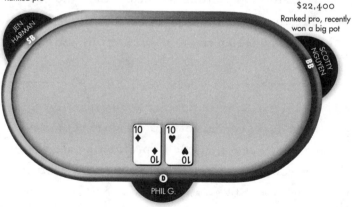

$32,000
Ranked pro

$22,400
Ranked pro, recently
won a big pot

JEN HARMAN SB

SCOTTY NGUYEN BB

10 ♦ / 10 ♥

Ⓓ PHIL G.

$27,400

POT: $3,900   **TO CALL:** $2,000   **POT ODDS:** 1.2–1

Scotty "You Call It's All Over, Baby" Nguyen is on a rush.

I don't believe in rushes, those incredible runs of good (or bad) luck when you can't seem to do anything wrong (or right.) I will admit, however, that rushes can often have a huge impact on the way I play a hand.

No, I'm not flip-flopping. While I don't believe in rushes from a *mathematical* perspective, I am often in awe of their power from a *psychological* perspective. I know that other people believe in rushes. Understanding an opponent's belief structure goes a long way toward predicting how that person is likely to play.

Let me be clear. I'm not accusing Scotty—a world champion and one of the toughest, most unpredictable poker players you'll ever encounter—of any sort of mental deficiency. I'm not even sure that he believes in rushes, at least not in any scientific way. But, like many other players, he has discovered that positive beliefs ("I'm *en fuego!*") do a lot more to help you win than negative beliefs do ("Why can't I win a damn hand?").

What I do know is that Scotty just won two big pots and that he's feeling incredibly optimistic about his chances. He just ordered another Corona. I just might be able to use that optimism against him.

I have pocket tens, a very good hand in a three-handed game—before the flop. Unfortunately, they are often very difficult to play *after* the flop, since overcards aren't just likely but probable. If you've ever raised with tens, only to see an A-K-8 flop, then you know exactly what I mean.

Heads-up and going all the way to the river, however, my tens are a favorite to beat anything that's not an overpair. In a three-handed game the odds of there being a bigger overpair out there are around one in twenty-five.

How should I play this hand? What would you do?

All night long I've been raising three times the big blind whenever I've been the first to enter the pot. What would happen if I were to vary that a bit and raise, say, four or five times the big blind? How would Scotty interpret that action? My guess is that he'd interpret it as weakness, a sign that I really don't want any action. In his current Superman-like state of mind, he might just make a move on me.

I think that $10,000, five times the big blind, feels about right. I slide my chips in and pray for action.

Jen folds quickly, and just as I'd hoped, Scotty

re-raises all-in. I call in a shot. His A♥8♦ is a decent but not great hand: I've got a better than 70% chance of winning. I close my eyes, and when the dealing's done, I've eliminated Scotty and built a very nice chip lead over Jen.

I think I'm on a rush!

❦ KEY ANALYSIS ❦

While I don't believe in rushes, I believe that other players do. When I think an opponent thinks he's on a rush, I do my best to give him a reason to make a big mistake.

I MAY NOT BE THE BEST PLAYER AT THE TABLE, BUT . . .

THE SITUATION: The final table at the 2001 *World Series of Poker* championship. Six players remain.

──POT LIMIT HOLD'EM TOURNAMENT──
Blinds $10,000/$20,000 with $3,000 antes

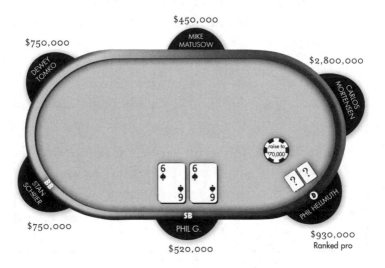

POT: $118,000 **TO CALL:** $60,000 **POT ODDS:** 1.2–1

I don't have to be the best player at the table. All I have to do to win is play better than a few of my opponents. Easier said than done at this final table, the last major championship table to feature more "pros" than "schmoes."

The best players in the world are the best players in the world for a lot of reasons. . . . Courage, genius, aggression, and perceptiveness all come to mind. But

296

the number one gift shared by almost every great player is the ability to adapt. It may take a hand, an hour, or a complete session, but the great player is going to figure out the style of poker you are playing. Fall into any kind of routine against a top pro, and he or she is going to make you pay.

Usually.

I'll admit that I wasn't very experienced in high-level competition going into the 2001 *WSOP* championship, but there was one "fact" that I'd discovered and exploited to great advantage—Phil Hellmuth Jr. doesn't like to call all-in raises, especially from cocky upstarts like me (then). Like most good players, Phil tries to steal the blinds whenever he can and "chip" his way through the field. Big conflicts are not his thing—why should he put all of his chips at risk, leaving himself vulnerable to a bad beat, against an opponent he can nickel-and-dime to death?

Hellmuth's strategy becomes expensive, however, when his opponents start playing back at him with big re-raises. It didn't take me long to discover that Phil was particularly vulnerable to this kind of counteraggression: He grudgingly folded to my all-in re-raises from the blinds many times during the first few hours at the final table. I was so proud of myself for picking up this tendency that I started showing him the kind of crap that I was re-raising him with.

Brilliant, Gordon. Truly brilliant.

Getting back to the hand in question . . . no, my pocket sixes aren't a particularly great hand, but you don't need a great hand to re-raise with all of your chips. Hellmuth isn't going to call me, anyway. And even if he does, I'm a slight favorite to win against two overcards. The odds are made even better by the nearly $120,000 that is already sitting in the pot. But as I said, he isn't going to call me, anyway.

What would you do?

Re-raise all-in, of course! Hellmuth isn't going to call! Take the free money in the pot! Show him another crappy "bluff" and tilt him some more!

Except that's not the way it turned out. Hellmuth later said in an interview: "I called his $450,000 raise so quickly that I freaked out everyone at the table. I just knew that he was going to move all-in with a weak hand, and this time I was ready for him."

The other Phil turned over 9-9. I was worse than a 4—1 underdog. I was an idiot. I was . . .

THE FLOP

. . . a legend of poker!

The turn and river failed to help the former world champion. I won the $1.2 million pot and crippled Hellmuth in the process. I watched him mutter to himself. Seething. Stewing. Cursing under his breath. The Tiltboys, several of whom were sitting in the audience, beamed with visible pride, not because of my play—a rookie, boneheaded mistake—but because of the incomparable result: I put a really bad, tilting beat on Hellmuth.

I don't have to be the best player at the table. I just have to be the luckiest.

❖ KEY ANALYSIS ❖

If you are going to mix it up with the best players at your table, be aware that they are likely to catch on to whatever strategies you're using to play them. They will eventually find a way to make you pay. (In theory, anyway. . . .)

UNEXPECTED FIREWORKS

THE SITUATION: The final (televised) table at the 2004 Bay 101 Shooting Stars tournament. Five players remain.

——NO LIMIT HOLD'EM TOURNAMENT——
Blinds $12,000/$24,000 with $3,000 antes

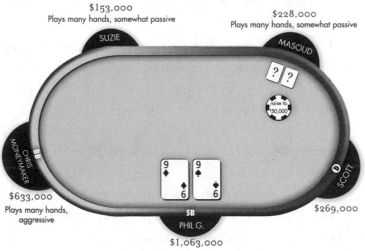

POT: $101,000 **TO CALL:** $38,000 **POT ODDS:** 2.7–1

So is Masoud strong or weak?

I'm always a little leery of the "mini-raise"—he's opted to enter the pot with a raise just above the minimum allowed—but in this case, with pocket nines and a million-plus in chips, the situation just looks too good. One of the great things about having a big stack is that I can play this hand without jeopardizing my standing. I'm definitely going to play. Should I call or should I re-raise?

What would you do?

I decide to make Masoud play for all his chips, re-raising to $278,000. I am concentrating so intently on Masoud's response that it takes me a few seconds to notice that Chris Moneymaker, the only player left to act behind me, is fumbling with his chips. The focus on the TV cameras tightens on the former world champion. I can feel the sweat pouring down my back. This is a critical pot. I just know that if I can win this pot and eliminate Masoud, I'll own the table and the title. I really don't want Chris to play.

Moneymaker thinks for what seems like two minutes before announcing, "I'm all in." Oh, man, not good. And worse . . . Masoud very quickly calls all-in.

I am completely disgusted.

There is $1.2 million in the pot. It will cost me $379,000 to call. I am getting about 3.2–1 to call for the big pot, and exactly even money on the side pot with Chris. Winning both pots would give me nearly all the chips, eliminate two tough opponents, and make for some good TV. Calling and losing, however, would put a huge dent in my chances to win the tournament.

I am getting good odds to call, especially for the side pot, but are they the right odds? I study my opponents. Chris isn't giving away any tells from behind his dark sunglasses. Masoud looks physically ill.

Aside from sweating all over the *WPT* cameras (as I did), what would you do?

Against two opponents—one who has raised all-in after a raise and a re-raise, and another who's willing to call that all-in bet—I am up against two overlapping sets of overcards, making me worse than a 4–1 underdog. Even if both players have lost their minds and I am up against two sets of overcards (A-K and A-Q, or A-Q and A-J), I would still be an underdog to win the pot (although I'd be getting the correct pot odds to call.) The only way I would be any kind of favorite to win the hand is if my two opponents happened to hold identical hands, like A-K, A-K.

I also have to consider the impact of calling (and

losing) on my chip stack. The average stack among the remaining players is about $500,000. My $278,000 re-raise has only dropped me to about $700,000, well above the average. If Chris or Masoud wins the pot, I'll no longer be the chip leader, but that is largely irrelevant compared with the dangers of calling another $379,000 and losing—I would fall to just over $300,000, well *below* the average, and I'd be in some serious trouble.

It's not an easy fold, but I think it is the best play. I toss my nines into the muck, trying to predict how the trolls on RGP (www.recpoker.com) and the other Internet newsgroups will describe my decision.

There is definitely a moment of coward's regret when I see the hands I was up against: Masoud had A♦J♦, Chris had A♥Q♥. I would have been about 42% to eliminate both players, and I definitely made a mistake—at least from an equity perspective—by folding against these hands.

The flop comes T-8-2 and I really want to crawl under the table. The turn card, a seven, doesn't make me feel much better. When the river brings a nine—making me a set—my legs get weak . . . until I realize that the card gives Masoud a straight. I would have lost the main pot.*

---

* Although it hardly would have been a disaster—the side pot would have allowed me to show a net profit on the hand, and Chris would have been eliminated.

Masoud moves into the chip lead, Chris takes his "bad beat" like a gentleman, and I have a long and hard battle ahead of me. . . .

In retrospect this was one of the most difficult decisions I've ever had to make at a final table. I felt like Chris was making a move, but I couldn't be sure. He would have made the same play, without a doubt, with pocket tens or better. I love his re-raise there—he got all his money into the pot with the best hand and plenty of dead money to boot. If a different river card had come, Chris would have had a commanding chip lead, on my left, with just four players left. The entire complexion of the tournament would have changed. As it was, I battled back to retake the chip lead and eventually win the tournament.

❖ KEY ANALYSIS ❖

When making decisions for large quantities of chips, be sure to consider the possible actions of the players left to act behind you, and think about how a multiway pot might affect your equity in the hand. In very close decisions lean toward the conservative action if that action will leave you below average in chips.

LIMPING

THE SITUATION: Heads-up against Jennifer Harman at the 2003 Ultimate Poker Classic in Aruba.

——NO LIMIT HOLD'EM TOURNAMENT——
Blinds $1,500/$3,000 with $500 antes

POT: $5,500   **TO CALL:** $1,500   **POT ODDS:** 3.7–1

I've been lucky enough to win a couple of pots against Jen, a friend who, I don't mind admitting, is a much better player than I am. Now I've got her outchipped and, with a very strong hand in good position, on the ropes. The question is how to play it.

What would you do?

If you've read *Little Green Book*—or even skimmed the table of contents—then you know that I like to raise when I am the first one in the pot. There are situations, however, when I think limping makes sense, but only when very shorthanded:

♣ **I have a strong hand and suspect my opponent may raise me.** Jen is an aggressive player sitting behind a small stack. She's looking for spots to move in with all of her chips—weakness, feigned or otherwise, may give her exactly what she's looking for.

♣ **The players in the blinds are weak after the flop.** This certainly isn't the case here, but if Jen does decide to raise me, it's likely to be for all of her chips. This will eliminate any chance she has to outplay me after the flop.

♣ **Limping will help deceive my opponents.** Trust me. Against Jen, I'll need all the deception I can get.

All in all, this is a pretty good spot to limp in from. I complete the blind. Jen takes a few seconds to consider her options, then raises me all-in.

What would you do?

Against players more skilled than you, there are worse things to do than get your money into the middle with a fifty-fifty shot at winning. You can't get outplayed when you let the poker gods determine your fate.

I call, hoping she has a weak ace, but her 6-6 actually makes her a slight favorite to win this particular "race." My lucky streak continues, however, when I catch a queen on the flop and my hand holds up to win.

In retrospect this might have been the most important race of my life, not to mention the effect it's had on _your_ life. If I hadn't won this hand, Jen would have been a heavy favorite to finish me off and take the title. Without that _WPT_ title, I might not have been asked to cohost _Celebrity Poker Showdown_. Without the show, I wouldn't have gotten the opportunity to write books. Without the books, well, you'd be reading the funny pages. And if you're one of the hundreds of thousands of players who have learned and improved from my poker writing, my A-Q versus Jen's 6-6 was a pretty important race in your own poker career!

While I almost always prefer to raise when I'm first to enter a pot, there are situations where limping in with a strong hand is a perfectly acceptable strategy. And against players who can consistently outplay you after the flop, don't be afraid to risk your chips on fifty-fifty propositions.

SIT & GOS

One of the more interesting phenomena associated with the online poker explosion has been the ubiquitous growth of Sit & Go tournaments, events with a limited number of seats that begin the moment all the seats get filled.

Sit & Gos force you to alter your strategy—invoking more or less the same thinking you'd apply to the beginning, middle, and end of a normal tournament—in a very compressed period of time, usually not more than an hour or two. As a result, they make great practice for longer events (not to mention one-table satellites), and you rarely have to wait more than a few minutes to join one!

I think that playing Sit & Gos is the best way to prepare yourself for the many challenges you'll face at the table in tournaments.

My strategy here mirrors my multitable strategy for the most part:

♥ Play tight in the early couple of levels of blinds.
♥ Look for weak-tight players and take advantage of them.
♥ Build a tight-aggressive image, and rarely if ever bluff in the early going.
♥ At about the fourth or fifth level go for a "big play" against the loose-aggressive types who play too many hands.
♥ When we're on the bubble, play hyperaggressively and steal many pots.
♥ When the bubble bursts and we're in the money (generally with three players remaining), I tighten up a bit if I'm the big stack. And I wait for highly profitable situations while the two short stacks do battle.

On FullTiltPoker.com I play these Sit & Go tournaments about three or four times a week under my own name. Come and give it a shot—I'll be more than happy to donate to your bankroll!

GETTING IT IN WITH THE BEST

THE SITUATION: Early in a $50 Sit & Go tournament at FullTiltPoker.com. Nine players remain.

──NO LIMIT HOLD'EM SIT-AND-GO──
Blinds $30/$60

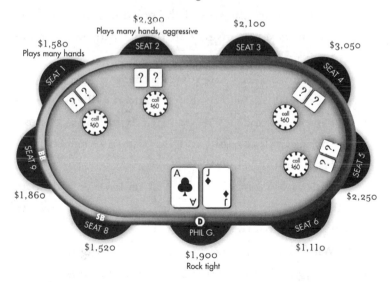

POT: $330   **TO CALL**: $60   **POT ODDS**: 5.5–1

A lot of players have been seeing a lot of flops in this one-table tournament, but not me. I've been sticking to my usual game plan of maintaining a tight image through the early stages of a tournament. In fact, I haven't played a hand yet.

That's about to change. . . . On the button against four limpers, none of whom are likely to have a powerful hand, I don't need great cards to try to take the pot with a raise. That I actually *have* a good hand is gravy.

How much would you raise?

I like to raise the size of the pot here, and the "Bet Pot" button is very convenient for that purpose. I make it $330 to go.

Everyone folds to the player in Seat 2, who re-raises all-in. There is $2,960 in the pot, and it will cost me the rest of my chips, or $1,570, to call. My options: Gamble with him and call, or fold and wait for a better spot.

What would you do?

This is No Limit Hold'em at its best: It has taken me five seconds to go from tight and conservative to making a decision for all my chips.

What could he have? He's been playing loose and wild, so just about anything is possible. A-K, A-Q? Not likely. I think he would have raised the first limper with those hands. A-J? Possible, but again, not likely. A medium pocket pair and a dentist appointment? That might do it. A chance to tell all his friends he bluffed Phil Gordon out before the flop? Priceless.

The pot is laying me nearly 2–1 odds, meaning that I have to win only around 33% of the time to make this a positive equity decision. I would be correct in calling against any pocket pair queens or lower (more or less a coin flip). Against A-K or A-Q, I'm making a small equity mistake. The only situation where I'd be wrong in calling—very wrong—is if he has pocket aces, which would give him a better than 90% chance of winning. I just don't think that's very likely.

I don't like it, but I think I have to call. I click the button. It takes less than a millisecond for all of my chips to reappear in the middle of the table.

Seat 2 turns over . . . K-9 offsuit. So much for my calculations! I'm about a 2–1 favorite to win more than $4,000 and take a commanding chip lead.

Alas, the maniac spikes the nine on the river. I'm broke but leave the table with the bittersweet feeling that I made the correct decision.

❖ KEY ANALYSIS ❖

All you can do is analyze each situation to the best of your ability and get your money into the pot with the best hand. The rest is up to the poker gods.

DRAWING BLANKS

THE SITUATION: Early in an online No Limit Hold'em Sit & Go at FullTiltPoker.com. Nine players remain.

——NO LIMIT HOLD'EM SIT-AND-GO——
Blinds $20/$40

POT: $100   **TO CALL**: $40   **POT ODDS**: 2.5–1

Per my usual, I have been playing squeaky tight during the early going of this tournament. I've been dealt a good hand, however, in position against a limper (let's call him "Limpy") who has been playing nearly every hand he's been dealt.

Should I call Limpy, or should I raise? What would you do?

I don't like calling here—with a very solid player to my immediate left, I don't want to give him good odds to call me in position. I also don't want the blinds to see the flop cheaply. A raise to $100 seems about right to me, and I do just that.

The dealer and the small blind fold, but the player in the big blind calls. So does Limpy. No surprise there. There is $320 in the pot.

——THE FLOP——

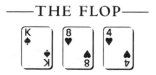

This is actually a pretty good flop for me. The cards aren't grouped closely together which, eliminates any legitimate draw at a straight, and should the board continue "flushing," I'll wind up with the nuts.

Both opponents check to me. My choices: bet or check. What would you do?

First of all I'm happy that no one bet in front of

me. My hand may very well be the best right now, and I think it's worth trying to pick up the pot with a continuation bet. Even if someone turns out to be ahead of me, I have nine outs to the nut flush, and six remaining aces and queens to improve my hand. With both of my opponents showing weakness, it seems clear to me to retain control of the betting and back up my preflop raise with a postflop continuation bet.

How big a bet should I make? I'm going to bet about two thirds of the pot, enough to make it look like I'm trying to protect my hand from a potential flush draw.

I bet $250. The big blind folds, but Limpy calls. There is $820 in the pot.

I'm not thrilled that Limpy called my bet. He probably has a better hand than I do. Maybe K-Q, K-J, pocket eights, or fours. Heck, a player as loose as this guy might even turn over a hand like A-4 or A-8.

——THE TURN——

The four isn't a bad card for me, because it's unlikely to have improved his hand. Then again, it didn't do much for my hand either.

Once again Limpy checks to me.

Another check? Something feels odd. Should I make another bet here, or take a free shot at improving on the river?

The Rule of Two tells me that I have about an 18% chance of making a flush on the river (9 outs x 2 = 18%), and a 30% chance of improving if an ace or queen is good. I'd be getting the right odds to make a small bet here, say, $200 or so, but I'll also be exposing myself to a difficult decision if Limpy decides to check-raise me. My superior position—not to mention the aggression I showed before and immediately following the flop—has earned me the chance to take a free card. I'm happy to take it here.

I check. The dealer burns and exposes the river card . . .

——THE RIVER——

Well, a heart would have been better, but there's a good chance the ace put me in the lead. The pair of fours on the board even protects me against a weird hand like K-8.

Limpy bets $400. There is $1,220 in the pot.

Huh? It's official—I have no idea what I'm up against. This betting just doesn't make sense. Maybe he was trying to check-raise me on the turn after making trip fours? He could have A-8, but that seems rather unlikely. He might also be making a desperate bid to bluff me out of the pot with a busted flush or gut-shot straight draw. One thing is certain: He's played this hand in a very strange way.

When a player who has been playing weakly throughout the hand suddenly comes to life on the river, I have to seriously consider the possibility that he's bluffing. I don't like that his bet is on the small side—it seems as if he wants me to call—but I'm getting better than 4–1 odds from the pot and I have top pair.

Raising on the river is clearly out of the question—the only way he's going to call is if he's got the better hand. So my options are clear: call or fold. What would you do?

If he was trying to reel me in, he has just succeeded.

I call the $400. Limpy turns over 8♣8♦. He flopped a set and improved to a full house on the turn.

A kick in the nuts and, as it turns out, a near-fatal blow for me. While I don't particularly like the way he played that hand—his weak play on the flop could easily have come back to bite him had the turn been a heart—I'll make a note of his slowplay for future reference. I'm down to about twelve big blinds, but I'm still alive. Time to get back to work!

❖ KEY ANALYSIS ❖

Drawing hands are difficult to play in No Limit Hold'em. Timely aggression and superior position can help defray some of the costs.

THE ANDREW END

THE SITUATION: Early in a $100 Sit & Go on FullTiltPoker.com. Nine players remain.

—NO LIMIT HOLD'EM SIT-AND-GO—
Blinds $25/$50

POT: $175 **TO CALL:** $0

I've got a decent hand with lots of potential in the big blind. I also have a massive early chip lead in this tournament. With two limpers, the action's on me. I can either click the "Check" button and see the flop for free or I can wield the big stack like a billy club and raise these limpers in an attempt to take the pot down right now. What would you do?

While this is a decent spot to try to steal the pot

by raising the limpers, there are (at least) four factors that suggest a more conservative approach for this hand:

1. I've been the most aggressive player at the table so far, and my opponents are less likely to give me credit for a great hand.
2. If one or both of them call, I'll be out of position throughout the hand.
3. There's not much chance my hand is the best right now, but the implied odds are very big.
4. I'm the chip leader, and the player in second place, FoolHouse, is in the pot.

Checking seems clear.

——THE FLOP——

A fantastic flop, and one that very likely has given me the best hand: Only A-K and K-9 beat me right now, though I do have the "dumb end" of the straight.* My

---

* My fiancée calls this the "Andrew end" of the straight. See opening Acknowledgments.

options: Check and go for the slowplay/check-raise, or bet right out.

What would you do?

As I said, unless someone has A-K or K-9, I have the best hand right now. A-K is almost completely out of the question—no one raised before the flop. There aren't any flush draws to beat me, but if the turn pairs the board or brings an ace, king, or nine, I am going to be somewhat unhappy.

I decide to bet out. With the dumb end of the straight, there are plenty of cards that can come that will not make me happy. My hand is never going to improve. I want to take this pot right away if possible.

How much would you bet?

Very often when I flop the dumb end of the straight against multiple opponents, I find that a bet of about the size of the pot is the right play. No reason to depart from the playbook here. . . . I bet $175. Poker Joker folds, but FoolHouse, perhaps living up to his name, unexpectedly raises to $600. There is $950 in the pot, and it will cost me $425 to call.

This just got interesting. What kind of hand could he possibly have for this raise?

I still don't think he limped in with A-K, but K-9 is a real possibility. The size of his raise doesn't give me much information to work with.

Did he flop a set? That would certainly be consistent with his overbet. But with a hand like Q-Q, J-J, or T-T, wouldn't he have raised before the flop?

He seems like a reasonably sane player, so his big bet really leaves only a few options: K-Q, K-J, Q-J, K-T, or K-9. If he has a king, I definitely do not want to see an ace or a nine come off the top of the deck. If he's got two pair, he has only a 17% chance of filling up by the river. All of these hands will be very difficult for him to get away from after he's invested so much money already. So, bottom line: I can call, or I can re-raise.

What would you do?

I want him to make a big mistake now. I re-raise to $2,000. He goes all-in for $3,150. There is $5,325 in the pot, and it will cost me $1,150 to call. Calling that bet is the easiest thing I've done in a week. If he's got K-9, well, he's about to double up.

I click "Call," and FoolHouse shows Q♣J♠ for two pair. All I have to do now is avoid another queen or jack.

The turn is the A♦, the river the 2♠. My straight holds on to win. Had I chosen to slowplay, this hand would have been much more difficult for me. After the ace came on the turn, my opponent would have been very careful about putting a lot of chips into the pot, and I would have been scared he had a king and the nut straight.

This was an outstanding result for me—I eliminated a tough player, won a huge pot, and gained a massive chip lead. This sit-and-go looks like it's mine for the taking.

❖ KEY ANALYSIS ❖

When you flop the "dumb" end of a straight, play with even more aggression than usual—there are too many cards that can counterfeit your hand or shut down an opponent's action.

TAKING IT DOWN ON THE TURN

THE SITUATION: A single table Sit & Go tournament at FullTiltPoker.com. Five players remain.

—NO LIMIT HOLD'EM SIT-AND-GO—
Blinds $50/$100

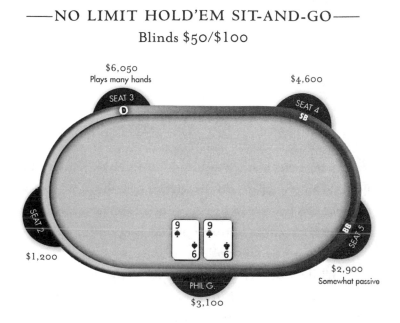

$6,050
Plays many hands

SEAT 3
D

$4,600

SEAT 4
SB

SEAT 2

$1,200

9♠ 6♠ 9♣ 6♣

BB
SEAT 5

$2,900
Somewhat passive

PHIL G.

$3,100

POT: $150   **TO CALL:** $100   **POT ODDS:** 1.5–1

Early on in a tournament I might consider limp-ing in with pocket nines hoping for a multiway pot. With only five players remaining, however, my nines become a raising hand, even under the gun.

I raise to $300. The button (a somewhat loose player) and the big blind (a somewhat passive player) both decide to call. There is $950 in the pot.

So much for picking up the blinds.

——THE FLOP——

Who cares about the blinds—I'm looking to double up! I do a little jig . . . on the inside. The big blind checks to me. I can bet out and pray for a call (or raise), or I can check and hope the button does my betting for me.

What would you do?

While I'll occasionally consider slowplaying a set when I'm out of position, there's no way I can afford to give my opponents a free card here, given this board's straight and flush possibilities.

What hands are my opponents likely to have? The big blind might have a big ace (although, I think he would have led out with a bet on the flop if he had A-Q) or pocket pair. The loose button might be playing a much wider range of hands—a low pocket pair or suited connector isn't out of the question. I'm worried about K-J, K-T, and J-T making a straight. I also don't want to give a free draw to a flush.

Do I push all-in? It's certainly an option. But at this point in the tournament, I need to extract the maximum number of chips possible. I definitely want action if someone has a pair of queens, and I can bet enough to give them incorrect odds to chase a straight or flush draw. Two thirds of the pot should be enough.

I bet $600. Both players call! There is $2,750 in the pot.

——THE TURN——

A great card for me. Unless someone was playing 8♦7♦, I'm almost certainly still ahead. The big blind checks to me.

What would you do?

There is $2,750 in the pot, and I have $2,200 left in my stack. Now is the time to move all-in. Just winning what is already in the middle will be enough to make me the chip leader—I don't have to milk any more out of this situation. Nor do I really mind if one or both of them call, as the size of my bet will be enough to ruin their odds if they're chasing flushes or straights.

I push all-in. Both players fold. I might have snapped the line on my fish, but I'm very happy to be the chip leader and in command of the table.

❖ KEY ANALYSIS ❖

Avoid overbetting hands on the flop, but when the pot gets big on the turn and you're confident that you have the best hand, do whatever you have to do to take it down.

REVERSAL OF FORTUNE

THE SITUATION: A single-table Sit & Go tournament on FullTiltPoker.com. Seven players remain.

—NO LIMIT HOLD'EM SIT-AND-GO—
Blinds $30/$60

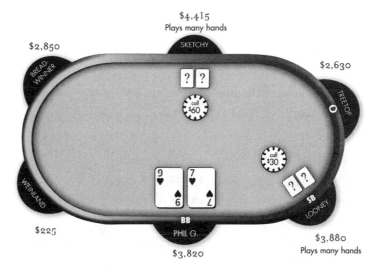

POT: $180   **TO CALL:** $0

When Sketchy and Looney limp into the pot, I give
some consideration to raising here in an attempt to take
the pot before the flop. But alas, getting a free look at the
flop with a suited one-gapper has to be a better idea.

I rap the table. There is $180 in the pot.

——THE FLOP——

Looney checks to me.

This is a great flop for me. Setting aside the obvious—any heart will give me a flush—the paired board makes it less likely that anyone caught a piece of the flop. In situations like this, the first player to make a bet often winds up with the pot. I like to bet a third to a half of the pot in these situations; I think $75 sounds about right here—the same bet, by the way, I'd make if I was holding a third eight.

I bet $75. Sketchy folds, but Looney check-raises me and makes it $200 to go. Very interesting. There is $455 in the pot, and it will cost me $125 to call.

Well, so much for that strategy. What could he have check-raised with here? Pocket eights or pocket fives seem unlikely—he'd probably have tried to slow-play either hand. He might have limped in with a hand like A-8, 9-8, or 8-7 and is now looking to protect his trips against the flush draw. Maybe he has A-5 or 6-5 and is "testing" me to see if I have an eight. I also have to consider the possibility that he doesn't believe that I have a piece of the board—that he read my smallish bet for weakness—and is trying to knock me off my "bluff."

Do I call here? I have nine outs to a flush and another three to a straight, or twelve outs to a hand that is likely to be a winner. Using the Rule of Two, I have about a 24% chance of getting there on the turn. My Break Even Percentage is $1 \div (3.6 + 1)$, or about 22%, so it's a close call.

What would you do?

The deciding factor for me, in the end, is that my opponent is an aggressive player who could be using "level two" thinking to make this raise—if I have nothing, he can raise me with anything. Calling here not only gives me the chance to make a winning hand, but if he is bluffing at the pot—even with a hand that happens to be better than my nine-high—I might have a chance to take it away from him on the turn.

I call his bet. There is $580 in the pot.

——THE TURN——

Looney leads out with a $500 bet. There is $1,080 in the pot, and it will cost me $500 to call.

The first bit of good news is that I'm pretty certain of what I'm up against—I'm almost sure he has trip eights.

How is that good news? Because if I know what he has, then I know what I need to beat him. This brings us to the second piece of good news—the jack adds a double gut-shot straight draw to my flush outs.

Nine flush outs plus another six nonsuited straight outs give me fifteen cards that can help me, although the paired board makes me more than a little nervous. He could already have a full house or, if he doesn't, draw to one with the same card I use to make my straight or flush.

What would you do?

Well, I think he has trips, and that pretty much eliminates any chance I will raise with this hand. I have yet to see an Internet player in a low-stakes tournament who is capable of laying down trips in a situation like this.

When deciding whether or not to call with a draw on the turn, I consider the implied odds—if I make my hand, will I get paid off on the river? I quickly run through the following checklist:

♠ Will my opponent call a big bet on the river? Hard to imagine him getting away from trips. A flush could scare him off, however, so let's call this one a "maybe."
♠ Do I believe he is strong but my draw will make me stronger? Yes.

♠ Are our stacks very deep? Not ridiculously so, but deep enough. If I call and miss my draw, I'll still have over $3,000, or more than fifty big blinds—well within my comfort zone. He's got me slightly outchipped, so if I call and draw to a winner, there's a chance I can double up.

♠ Do I have a deceptive draw? Not in regards to the flush, but a definite "yippee" on the well-concealed double gut-shot draw. The safe answer here is "it depends."

♠ Has my draw been telegraphed? I certainly hope not. I came out betting on the flop, and didn't back down when he raised. My hope is that he is putting me on a five or a weaker eight than his.

♠ Is my opponent an expert? We're playing on the Internet. My opponent could be Johnny Chan . . . or it could be my eight-year-old nephew. There's no way to know for sure.

Sifting through the evidence, I think that I can make a reasonable case for calling here.

I call. There is $1,580 in the pot.

——THE RIVER——

The river is a complete blank, and I have no chance to win the pot without a bet. Looney checks to me. Do I risk the bluff, or check and concede the pot?

What would you do?

It's tempting, but I think I'm better off sticking to my original read: He has an eight, and probably isn't going to throw away his hand. In fact, his check here seems very much like an attempt to induce a bluff from me.

I check. Looney turns over A♠8♠ for three of a kind. I muck my busted draw.

I didn't win the pot, but I don't hate the way I played the hand; I put myself in a very good position to take all of his chips without jeopardizing my chances to win the tournament.

❦ KEY ANALYSIS ❦

Playing draws can be tricky in No Limit Hold'em. Your decisions are often based less on current pot odds than on implied odds and the deceptiveness of your draw. Also, recognize that a check on the river can mean weakness or strength in an effort to induce a bluff—trusting your read is the key to knowing which it is more likely to be.

MAD MONEY

THE SITUATION: Early in a one-table Sit & Go on FullTiltPoker.com. Nine players remain.

—NO LIMIT HOLD'EM SIT-AND-GO—
Blinds $20/$40

$615
Recently lost a big pot

$1,500

$1,045

ANGRY-GUY
SB

BUDDHA
BB

$3,180

CONSTANCE
D

MATTY

ROBBIN

raise to $80

? ?

BUNCHED

$3,060
Plays many hands, aggressive

$1,470

DON_JUAN

PHIL G.

HURLEY

$1,755
Somewhat tight

$1,390

$3,845

POT: $140   **TO CALL:** $80   **POT ODDS:** 1.8–1

It's been a lively tournament, to say the least. In a clear example of poetic justice—or at least of players living up to their screen names—Robbin just laid a bad beat on AngryGuy. The chat box has been busy.

Sometimes it's better to be sitting outside the fray when things get this volatile, but the poker gods have other plans for me. I'm not going to throw away A-K here. This is a clear-cut re-raise situation, I think, and I'm going to re-raise somewhere between three and four times the size of my opponent's bet.

I re-raise to $250. I'm shocked and pleasantly surprised to see AngryGuy call from the small blind. The initial raiser, Bunched, decides to call as well. There is $790 in the pot.

——THE FLOP——

AngryGuy angrily leads out with a $40 bet. Bunched quickly calls. There is $870 in the pot, and it will cost me $40 to call.

What would you do?

This is either a great situation (a tilting player helping to build a nice pot for me) or I'm in huge trouble (one of these two guys is softplaying a monster hand and laying a trap for me).

I'm not that worried about AngryGuy. He's got enough chips to put a small dent in my stack but not enough to make me consider folding my hand. If he's got me beat, I'm fully prepared to double him up. As for Bunched, well, unless he's slowplaying, he probably would have raised AngryGuy's bet with anything resembling a decent hand.

Obviously, I have to raise. The key here is to choose an amount that forces AngryGuy to make a decision for all of his chips and wipes out the odds for Bunched to call with a potential draw.

Further complicating matters is the likelihood that AngryGuy, who is pretty much pot committed if he's got any kind of hand with a chance of winning, is going to call my bet. While betting a third of the current pot might *seem* like enough to force Bunched off a flush draw, should AngryGuy call the bet, Bunched will actually be getting the right odds to continue.

This situation is sort of the inverse of a traditional implied odds scenario: I need to bet enough money to ruin the odds that Bunched will be facing should AngryGuy call my bet.

There is $870 in the pot. AngryGuy has $345 left. Assuming he puts that money into the pot, there will be $1,215. If I bet $405 and AngryGuy calls, Bunched will have 4–1 odds to call, or exactly what he needs to chase a flush. Betting a little more—say, $450 or so—will make it incorrect for him to call unless he's got some kind of straight-flush combination.

I raise to $500, enough to put AngryGuy all-in. He obliges, as I'd expected. Bunched takes about fifteen seconds, but finally folds.

AngryGuy turns over K♥J♦. You've got to love a guy on tilt—he's called off all of his chips against a hand (my hand) that has had him dominated from the start. He needs one of the three jacks left in the deck (or a running Q-T) to beat me.

The turn is the 7♠, the river the 6♠. I take the pot, and AngryGuy has the rest of the afternoon to stew.

❧ KEY ANALYSIS ❧

Don't call preflop raises with hands that are easily dominated, especially when you're on tilt. Be aware that after the flop, when you bet and get called, a third player will often be getting the right odds to chase a draw. In multiway pots it's generally a good idea to bet more than you would in an equivalent heads-up situation.

SATELLITES AND SUPERSATELLITES

Want to know why tournaments like the *World Series* and *World Poker Tour* have grown so huge? It's not that television has suddenly caused otherwise sane people to lose their minds and cough up the huge entry fees. Most of the players in the $10,000 buy-in tournaments win their way in through satellites and supersatellites. These tournaments allow you to risk a relatively small amount of money in the hopes of winning entry into a bigger buy-in event. Without the satellite system, players like Chris Moneymaker might never have had the chance to showcase their talents on poker's biggest stages.

The primary difference between satellites and "regular" tournaments is that you aren't looking to win money—you are looking to win a seat. As a result, you have to tailor your play to the format of the event. Playing for a single seat? You're probably going to have to play far more aggressively than normal, as there is no reward for second place—you've got to win to get in. On the other hand, an event that offers multiple seats might lead you to play far more conservatively, avoiding risky confrontations when it looks as if you have a chance of outlasting a few short-stacked opponents.

These tournaments are a great way to learn the game. If you get lucky, like I did in 2001 when I won a seat to the world championship event at the *World Series of Poker* in the very last satellite, you can find yourself sitting at the tables with Ivey, Lederer, Ferguson . . . and maybe me.

GUT-SHOT DREAMS

THE SITUATION: A single-table satellite—the winner receives entry to the *World Series of Poker* championship event. Three players remain.

——NO HOLD'EM SIT-AND-GO——
Blinds $100/$200

$5,100

SEAT 1

$4,900
Plays many hands,
aggressive

SEAT 2

SB

call
$100

?-?

J♠ 8♦

BB
PHIL G.

$3,500

POT: $400   TO CALL: $0

When everyone folds to the small blind, who just completes the bet, I give at least passing consideration to raising from the big blind. Two options: Check and see the flop for free, or raise and put some pressure on.

What would you do?

In this case I am facing a tricky and aggressive opponent. I've already seen him limp in with strong hands several times in this tournament, only to re-raise after someone's raised behind him. I'll just check here and see if I can use my position to outplay him on the flop.

I check. There is $400 in the pot.

——THE FLOP——

Not a particularly good flop for me. All I have is an overcard and a gut-shot straight draw. I am probably done with this hand. My opponent seems to study the board for a while before reaching into his stack for chips, returning with $200. There is $600 in the pot, and it will cost me $200 to call. I'm getting 3–1 on the call.

My options: raise and try to take the pot away, call and hope to spike a nine on the turn, or fold and save my money. What would you do?

If someone were taking side wagers, I'd bet my left foot that this guy has a good hand he is trying to disguise. Consider the evidence:

♦ He pretended to consider the board, a definite tell. He wants to seem weak when he is actually strong.

♦ He made the minimum bet on the flop, as if he's begging me for a raise or call.

My guess is that he has at least a pair of tens, and maybe even a set. I give myself an imaginary gold star for recognizing his trap. I start to throw my cards in the muck, when I see the potential for a different play.

Obviously, if I'm right in my read, raising here is akin to suicide. But what happens if I call? A nine will fill my gut-shot straight, almost certainly giving me the best hand. With four nines in the deck, I can use the Rule of Two to determine that I have about an 8% chance of filling my straight on the turn. The pot is laying me 3–1 odds, meaning that I have to win this hand 25% of the time for a call to be correct.

Or do I? If I did happen to spike a nine, it would be incredibly hard for him to put me on a straight. I'd have a very good chance of getting him to risk all of his chips, allowing me to win another $3,300 from him on the turn. Do my implied odds justify a call?

Implied odds = [($600 in the pot + $3,300 I'll get from him later) ÷ ($200 + $0 I'll have to call in the future)]−1 = 19.5−1.

My implied Break Even Percentage is about 5%. I've already determined that I have an 8% chance of catching my "gin card" on the turn. From a strictly mathematical perspective, calling doesn't look like such a bad idea anymore. While I'd never make this play with a short stack, the $200 it will take to call won't really affect my standing to any great extent. I'm speculating just about as much as it's possible to speculate at a poker table, but I think the potential rewards make it worthwhile.

I call the $200 and start praying for a nine on the turn. The pot contains $800.

——THE TURN——

The turn card doesn't help me a bit. My opponent, perhaps sensing my draw, perhaps scared of the "flushing" board, bets the pot, $800. I can fold, or I can continue chasing the straight. What would you do?

Well, clearly, I'm not getting the right pot odds: only 2–1. I'm also not getting the right implied odds. Folding has to be the right play, and I make the right play.

My opponent shows his hand with pride: Q-J. My read was completely wrong! That said, he was "bluffing" with the best hand.

❖ KEY ANALYSIS ❖

When considering whether or not to call a bet, the actual pot odds only tell part of the story. . . . Be sure to consider your implied odds, or how much money you will actually stand to win or lose by the end of the hand.

OFF TO THE RACES

THE SITUATION: The final table at a multitable satellite online at FullTiltPoker.com. Four players remain. Only the first-place finisher wins entry to a $10,000 buy-in *WSOP* Circuit event.

——NO LIMIT HOLD'EM SIT-AND-GO——
Blinds $1,000/$2,000 with $300 antes

$61,950

OLD-STOGEY

D

$29,150
Somewhat tight,
straightforward

LOONEY

SB

raise to
$7,000

WILEY
WABBIT

$15,400

BB
PHIL G.

$28,500

POT: $10,200   **TO CALL:** $5,000   **POT ODDS:** 2.0–1

This satellite is a winner-take-all affair, which makes winning the only thing that matters—second place pays the exact same as hundredth place. This suits me just fine; I always play to win. I've got some work to do, however, if I want to catch the chip leader, whose stack is more than twice as big as mine. Add to the mix that the blinds are relatively large in relation to our stack sizes. I'm going to have to be even more aggressive than usual.

Looney is a pretty straightforward player who doesn't really want to tangle with me. In the last four orbits he's surrendered his small blind to me three times. On the fourth occasion, he just completed the blind. He's raising now, so I have to give him credit for a decent hand. By "decent" I mean I can pretty much put him on one of the following:

♣ Any pocket pair
♣ Any ace
♣ K-Q or K-J

My A-Q in this situation is a great hand. If I choose to re-raise, the only play that really makes sense is to move all-in. So, here we are: call, all-in, or fold?

What would you do?

If I go all-in and he calls, I will have invested my entire $28,500 in the hopes of raking in a $58,200 pot. I'll be getting pot odds of about 1.04–1. My Break Even Percentage is about 49%. Those are about the right odds to take my A-Q against any pocket pair that isn't A-A, K-K, or Q-Q. I'm a big favorite against any ace except A-K (with A-Q being a wash), and a nice favorite over any other "decent" hand.

In situations like these I occasionally like to enumerate the range of my opponent's possible starting hands. It helps me see what I might be up against:

	The Good	Coin Flips	The Ugly
	A-J: 12	J-J: 6	A-A: 3
	A-T to A-2: 108	T-T to 2-2: 54	K-K: 6
	K-Q: 12	A-Q: 9	Q-Q: 3
	K-J: 16		A-K: 12
TOTALS:	148	69	24

What does this all mean? Well, of the 241 hands that I'm likely to be facing, I'm favored to win against 61% of them. I'm about even (or an ever-so-slight underdog) against 29% of the hands. I will be a substantial underdog only about 10% of the time.

It's a gamble, but it seems like an excellent opportunity to gather a lot of chips. I push all-in.

"Sweet," types Looney into the chat box as he calls my bet. He turns over pocket sevens, and the race is on.

He is about a 55-45 favorite to win, not what I'd call "sweet," but maybe that's why he's called Looney.

I don't pair my ace or queen, and I'm eliminated from the tournament. While I'm miserable now, I know I'll wake up tomorrow grateful that I played to win and went down swinging.

❧ KEY ANALYSIS ☙

While I'm not a big fan of gambling on "coin flips" early in a tournament, I am fully prepared to take more substantial risks later in a tournament when I am playing to win. As the blinds rise, so does my willingness to gamble.

COLLUSION COLLISION

THE SITUATION: The last supersatellite tournament to the 2000 *WSOP* main event. Eight players remain. The top seven finishers win seats.

──NO LIMIT HOLD'EM SIT-AND-GO──
Blinds $1,000/$2,000 with $300 antes

POT: $5,400   **TO CALL:** $2,000   **POT ODDS:** 2.7–1

Want to feel pressure? There are eight players left in this tournament. Seven are going to get to play in the World Series championship. One is going home.

The most likely outcasts are the two short stacks—the kid in Seat 3 with the UNLV sweatshirt, and Mieke, the drop-dead gorgeous blonde from Australia who's been throwing some interesting looks my way all night from Seat 5. And I'm not even famous yet. *Celebrity Poker Showdown* won't find its way onto the air for another three years or so.

I'm under the gun with a premium hand, A-K. What should I do? What would you do?

I am giving serious consideration to folding this hand. What! Am I crazy, or just a huge wimp? I hope neither. Although A-K is a great hand, there is no way I'm going to risk all my chips here with a full table left to act behind me, including two short stacks ready to go broke. Because of the format of the supersatellite, I'm not playing to win. I'm playing to finish seventh. The smart play is probably to fold my hand and watch the short stacks squirm as the blinds catch up with them.

Alas, folding A-K isn't in my playbook, at least not the circa-2000 version. Since my raise will get substantial respect due to my position, my stack size, and the situation, I decide to raise just two-and-a-half times the big blind.

I raise to $5,000. UNLV re-raises all-in, making it $30,000 to go. Surprisingly, David Plastik—the only pro at the table—just calls. And it may be my imagination, but David seems to wink at me as he puts his chips into the middle. Nothing personal, buddy, but I'm holding out for Mieke. There is $69,400 in the pot, and it will cost me $25,000 to call.

What would you do?

I go into my decision-making routine:

351

♥ **Do I re-raise?** A re-raise here would essentially force me to commit all of my chips to this pot. David will be getting better than 2–1 odds to call my bet, making it very hard for him to let his hand go.

♥ **Do I fold?** I am getting nearly 3–1 odds from the pot, and I'm holding A-K—hardly chopped liver. I don't think that folding is the right play. I can call the bet, lose the pot, and still have thirty big blinds. No, folding can't be right.

When I shouldn't raise and I shouldn't fold, calling starts to seem like a pretty good option.

I call the $25,000 and see the flop. There is $94,400 in the pot. A motley crew of parents, siblings, and significant others are on the rail holding their breath. If we can bust UNLV, we're all going to the big dance.

——THE FLOP——

Bingo! Take that, UNLV! The only place this Rebel is going to be running is all the way home.

David yells "CHECK" in an odd, almost stentorian tone. Everyone in the room is staring at me.

What would you do?

I rise from the table and announce I'm all-in. David's face turns beet red and the veins in his neck are straining to push through his skin. What did I do? I look to Mieke for encouragement, but she's buried her face in her hands, refusing to look at me. Don't they know I have top pair, top kicker?

David throws two black queens, faceup, into the muck. "F-ing Tiltboy," he mutters. I turn over my A-K. UNLV shows two black tens. Sweet! I've got him drawing to two outs.

——THE TURN——

UNLV and his fraternity brothers on the rail erupt in applause and cheers. I want to cry.

——THE RIVER——

As I look at the river card—and UNLV, adding my chips to his—I realize that I've made a terrible mistake. My bet forced David to throw away what would have been the winning hand. He wasn't going to add any more chips to the pot, and neither should I have. The only thing that really mattered was busting UNLV. David was banking on the fact that I understood the concept of "implicit collusion." It would have made far more sense for us both to have checked our hands down to the river, increasing our collective chances of eliminating UNLV and locking up our seats to the *WSOP*.

Just a few hands later Mieke busts out. I try to catch her eye, but she brushes right past me. Looks like my poor play busted my chances with her as well.

❧ KEY ANALYSIS ❧

There is nothing unethical (or unreasonable) about using "implicit collusion" late in a tournament or satellite to increase the chances of eliminating a short-stacked opponent.

A SLAM DUNK

THE SITUATION: The final table of an online satellite at FullTiltPoker.com. The winner receives a seat at a *WSOP* event. Five players remain.

—NO LIMIT HOLD'EM SIT-AND-GO—
Blinds $1,000/$2,000 with $300 antes

POT: $12,300   **TO CALL:** $5,800   **POT ODDS:** 2.1–1

During the early stages of a tournament, I play to stay alive, avoiding all-in coin flips and other situations where I have to risk a big chunk of my stack on a very close equity decision.

Late in a tournament, however, I don't have the same flexibility. The scenario in front of me is a perfect example. In order to call this all-in bet, I'll have to gamble nearly one fourth of my stack. The upside, however, is tremendous.

Winning this hand would eliminate an opponent and move me into a near-tie for the chip lead. Losing the hand would diminish my stack from about thirteen and a half to about ten and a half big blinds. It would hurt, but it wouldn't make my situation too much worse than it already is. If I'm getting the right odds to call, this is a pretty good spot to gamble.

Should I call? Am I getting the right odds? What would you do?

Because Basketballer has less than four big blinds, he's apt to push all-in here with a fairly wide range of hands—any pocket pair, any ace, a king or a queen with a face card kicker, and maybe even a few hands that are worse.

Of my opponent's likely hands, I have to be "afraid" of only the ones that have aces. Against A-A, I'm about a 7–1 underdog—ouch!—and any Ax hand (unless he has the same measly kicker as mine) will have me dominated. However, there are two bits of good news: (1) I'm holding an ace, which makes it a little less likely for him to have a hand with an ace in it, and (2) even if I'm dominated, I'm not as bad off as you might think—I'd be a 2.3–1 underdog to his hand, not so far removed from the 2.1–1 I'm getting from the pot. Against any other pocket pair, I'll be a 2.1–1 underdog and will be getting exactly the right odds to call. Against any other hand, I should be at least a 1.4—1 favorite to win.

So even though I am probably not favored to win this hand, I think it's reasonable to call in this situation.

Which I do. He turns over a big hand—K♠K♦—a 2.1—1 favorite to beat me. He has a very good chance of winning the hand, but the pot odds did justify my decision to call.

I catch an ace on the turn and eliminate Basketballer from the tournament.

❧ KEY ANALYSIS ❧

While it's usually best to avoid high-risk, high-reward situations during the early stages of a tournament, you are going to have to take a few chances during the late stages if you hope to win. There's nothing wrong with calling an all-in bet when you have a bigger stack and the correct pot odds to face off against your opponent's likely range of starting hands.

BROKEBACK MOUNTAIN

THE SITUATION: A satellite to a *WSOP* event. The top four finishers earn seats. Six players remain.

——NO LIMIT HOLD'EM SIT-AND-GO——
Blinds $1,000/$2,000

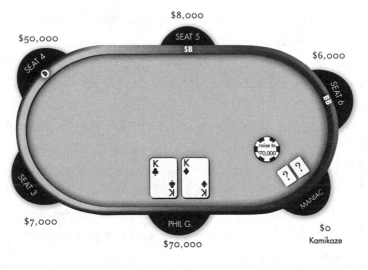

POT: $73,000   **TO CALL:** $70,000   **POT ODDS:** 1–1

A complete and total maniac, probably on furlough from the Las Vegas loony bin, pushes all-in with a huge stack from under the gun. Why he would do that as opposed to, say, raising to $8,000 (enough to put any of our three short-stacked opponents all-in) I have no idea.

And I've just woken up with cowboys. Two kings.

What would you do?

Were this a cash game, or even a "normal" tournament, my decision would be an easy one. Unless my opponent is holding pocket aces (and if he were, why would he be raising all-in before the flop?), I am a favorite to win and am clearly getting the right pot odds to call with all of my chips. I'd beat the maniac to the pot and feel great about doing so.

In this particular satellite, however, my goal isn't to win all of the chips. With four seats up for grabs, all I have to do is outlast two of my opponents. And three of them are in critical condition, clinging to life with four big blinds or fewer.

As much as I'd like to bust this yahoo for doing something so stupid, it just isn't worth the risk. In this spot I can probably just fold my way to the money. Pocket kings are a great hand, but against a hand like A-5, I'm only a 2—1 favorite to win, meaning I'll go broke 33% of the time. Why expose myself to that kind of chance? It looks like it's time for these cowboys to lie down.

I fold my kings. One of the short stacks in late

position calls with 9-9. The maniac turns over A-Q and wins when he spikes an ace on the river.

Think about this hand again. Would you make the same laydown with A-A? I know it seems strange, but all things considered, I just might!

❖ KEY ANALYSIS ❖

Regardless of the odds, you are going to take your share of bad beats. Just remember that a bad beat can't break you if you're never all-in against a bigger stack. Supersatellites on the bubble create very special situations: You're no longer trying to win chips or make the highest positive-equity plays; you're trying to survive and let the short stacks bust out.

HEAVENLY SEVENS

THE SITUATION: Heads-up at the final table of a charity tournament. The winner gets a free ticket to the *World Series of Poker*.

—NO LIMIT HOLD'EM SIT-AND-GO—

Blinds $20,000/$40,000 with $5,000 antes

$2,214,000
Beginner, kamikaze,
recently won a big pot

MOOSE

D

? ?

call
20,000

BB
PHIL G.

$876,000
On tilt, recently lost a big pot

POT: $90,000   **TO CALL:** $0

I am on tilt.

Nothing new here. My friends will tell you (half in jest, I hope) that I'm *always* on tilt. This time, however, I actually have a reason. On the previous hand, I managed to trick Moose, a lucky amateur, into getting all of his money into the middle with a hand I had dominated. All that stood between me, the title, and the first-place payday were three measly outs. He sucked out on the turn.

361

My more aggressive instincts—the ones that tilting tends to bring to the forefront—scream at me to raise a player who has merely completed the bet to see a cheap flop, but I have a trio of pretty good reasons to curb these instincts:

1. I'll be playing this hand out of position after the flop.*
2. I have a relatively small stack: I don't want to get myself into a position where my raise commits me to call a re-raise from Moose, a scenario where I'll probably wind up gambling all my chips with a very weak hand.
3. He knows I'm on tilt.

I check and wait for the flop.

——THE FLOP——

I seem to remember being angry about something a second ago. . . . What was it again? Who cares? I just

---

* In heads-up play the player with the button has to post the small blind and act first before the flop. After the flop, however, the player on the button receives the usual positional advantage of acting last.

flopped the nuts! Do I bet out and hope that Moose raises? Or do I slowplay and hope to trap him?

What would you do?

If this were earlier in the tournament, I'd probably make a small bet here hoping that he'd raise me. But given that I'm heads-up against an opponent who can afford to be very patient, there's a good chance that a bet here will frighten him off. Against an aggressive player like Moose, my goal is to slowplay just enough to give him enough rope to hang himself.

I check. He bets $45,000. I pretend to puzzle over my cards for a few seconds before calling. There is $180,000 in the pot.

——THE TURN——

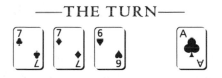

Now what? I could just check here and hope that Moose takes another stab at the pot . . . or, better yet, has an ace and pushes all-in! I'm in a unique position, however, to take advantage of my "tilting" image by "bluffing" at the pot. If I lead out with a bet here, what will Moose think I have? He might think that if I had had an ace in my hand I would have raised before the flop.

With a little luck, Moose will interpret my bet as a feeble attempt to steal the pot from him and he'll give me a little action.

I bet $90,000, and Moose re-raises all-in.

I'd like to say I expected *that* to happen, but I'd be lying. Unless he's holding pocket aces, Moose just handed me a golden opportunity to double up. I'll be sure to write him a thank-you note later using one-syllable words so as not to confuse him.

I quickly call his bet. Moose shows A♥T♥ and is drawing to just two outs. The river is a blank, I double up and regain the chip lead, and I'm ready to butt horns with the Moose.

❖ KEY ANALYSIS ❖

Against an aggressive opponent prone to bluffing and/or overbetting the pot, slowplaying can be a valuable tool. So is the ability to recognize and exploit your table image.

AFTERWORD

As I said at the beginning, there's no "correct" way to play a hand of poker. Changing conditions force changing strategies. The best players are the ones who know how to analyze the conditions and adapt accordingly.

I hope that this insight into the way I have approached certain hands will help you to better develop your own analytical talents. Yes, a lot of winning poker involves courage and luck, but careful study and thought will almost always put you in a better position to maximize your wins and minimize your losses.

If you find yourself wanting to study more of the

same, you may want to check out www.expertinsight.com, where you can pick up my *Final Table Poker* DVD or sign up for one of my Las Vegas Academy seminars. You can also often find me playing alongside some of the top pros in the world online at FullTiltPoker.com.

I hope to see you soon, whether at a seminar, online, or at a final table with millions of dollars on the line. Until then, I wish you the best of luck!

FURTHER STUDY

Many of the concepts I've used to play the preceding hands are developed in far more detail in my *Little Green Book*. For readers interested in brushing up on (or delving deeper into) these ideas, I've included a list below of specific page references to the sections in the *Little Green Book* that best apply to each hand.

CASH GAMES

Aloha, Full House!
"Pocket Pairs in Multiway Pots," p. 54

EARLY TOURNAMENT PLAY

MIDDLE TOURNAMENT PLAY

LATE TOURNAMENT PLAY

THE FINAL TABLE

SIT & GOS

SATELLITES AND SUPERSATELLITES

A SHORT GUIDE TO POKER JARGON

aggressive	The natural inclination to bet or raise, a hallmark of most winning poker players. The opposite of **passive**.
all-in	To call a bet with whatever you have left in front of you (as opposed to, say, the deed to the family ranch).
ante	A mandatory contribution to the pot, made by all the players at the table, before the cards are dealt.
backdoor flush	A flush completed by running cards on the **turn** and the **river**. Also called a **runner-runner flush**.
bad beat	An agonizing loss that defies the laws of logic and/or probability.
bad-beat story	The ensuing tale about just how bad a beat you were delivered, generally of interest only to the teller.
big blind	A mandatory bet posted before the cards are dealt, usually by the player two seats to the left of the dealer.

blind	A mandatory bet posted before the cards are dealt, intended to create a pot worth contesting. The term also refers to the player sitting in the blind position. See **small blind** and **big blind**.
board	The five community cards shared by the entire table.
board texture	The general "feel" of the community cards, which allows an observant player to get a sense of what hands his or her opponents might be holding.
boat	A full house.
bottom pair	When a **hole card** pairs with the lowest card on the **board**. For example, you are holding A-3, and the flop comes K-7-3.
Break Even Percentage (BEP)	The percentage of the time that you need to win a hand, in relation to the amount of money in the pot, to make a call worthwhile. BEP = 1 ÷ (Pot odds + 1)

bubble	The critical moment in a tournament when outlasting a handful of opponents will get you into the prize money, final table, etc.
button	The seat occupied by the **dealer**, or the player who gets to act last during each round of postflop betting.
buy-in	The amount of money required to sit down to a ring game or tournament.
calling station	A player easily exploited for his or her exaggerated tendency to call too many bets.
connectors	Two consecutive cards in the **hole**, (e.g., 7-6). This situation increases the odds of making a straight.
crying call	The act of calling a bet despite the near certainty that your hand is a loser. A common response to a **bad beat** or **suckout**.
cutoff	The seat just to the right of the **button**.

dead money	The aggregate of inferior players who have little to no chance of actually winning.
dealer	See **button**.
double gut-shot	A straight draw that isn't **open-ended** but that can still be completed by two different cards. For example, you hold 9-7 and the flop comes J-8-5. Any T or 6 will make you a straight.
doubling up	A won pot that doubles your current **stack**, the desired result of pushing **all-in** in a tournament.
drawing dead	The act of pursuing a **drawing hand**, unaware that even if you make it, you're still going to lose.
drawing hand	A hand that's not quite there yet but that could be if the right card or cards fall.
early position	Used to describe the players who are among the first to act before the flop. Early-position players will often face a positional disadvantage after the flop and usually limit themselves to a narrow range of good starting hands.

expected value	The profit or loss that a certain strategy or game will generate, on average, over the long run.
fancy play syndrome (FPS)	An expensive tendency, especially evident in players who have just read Sklansky and Malmuth, to overuse "trick" plays like check-raising or semibluffing.
fish	A bad player.
flat-call	To merely call a raise, usually from a superior position. Also called **smooth-call**.
flop	In Texas Hold'em, the first three community cards, dealt simultaneously.
fold equity	The chance that a bet or raise will get an opponent to fold a better hand than yours.
gut-shot	A straight draw that can be completed by only one card in the middle. Also called a **belly-buster**.
hand selection	The notion, ignored by many new or undisciplined poker players, that certain hands are more profitable than others.

heads-up	The moment when only two players remain to contest a hand or a game.
hole cards	The two "hidden" cards dealt to each player.
implied pot odds	A calculation of **pot odds** based not on the money that's currently in the pot but on the total money you anticipate will be in the pot at the end of the hand.
implicit collusion	An unspoken agreement between two or more players to check a hand down to the river after another player has already moved all-in. This increases the odds of eliminating the all-in player.
implied tilt odds (ITO)	The extremely scientific measure of the odds that a horrible decision will cause your opponent to explode in a fit of irrational rage.
junk	A hand that, at least according to poker mathematicians, should never be played. Also called **rags**.

kicker	The second card in the hole that is not used to make your hand but that might come into play to break a tie. For example, you hold A-K, your opponent holds A-J, and the final board looks like this: A-Q-9-9-3. Your hand—A-A-9-9-K—beats your opponent's A-A-9-9-Q.
late position	Used to describe the players who will have the best position after the **flop**—in a full game, the **cutoff** and the **button**. Late-position players get to act last (or second-to-last) after the flop, which allows them to play a much wider range of hands.
laydown	The act of folding one's hand. A "good" laydown occurs when you fold in a tough spot to a hand that turns out to have you beaten.
level one thinking	The act of judging the strength of your hand in order to make a decision.
level two thinking	The act of judging the strength of your opponent's hand in order to make a decision.

level three thinking	The act of using your opponent's likely assessment of the strength of your hand in order to make a decision.
limp	To enter a pot before the **flop** without raising.
loose	The willingness to see flops with a wider than average assortment of hands. The opposite of **tight**.
middle position	Used to describe the players seated between **early position** and **late position**.
monster	A very powerful hand.
muck	The pile of discards in the center of the table; also, the act of tossing your hand into said pile.
nuts	The best possible hand, given a particular **board**.
offsuit	Two **hole cards** of different suits, the opposite of **suited**.
open-ended	A straight draw consisting of four consecutive cards that can be completed by a card on either end. For example, you hold 7-6, and the flop comes J-5-4.

out	A card that, if dealt, will improve your hand.
overbet	The act of risking more money than you should to win a relatively small pot.
overcard	A card on the board that is higher than the cards in your hand, creating the potential that an opponent has a pair that's better than yours.
overpair	A **pocket pair** bigger than the highest card on the board. For example, you hold Q-Q and the flop comes 10-8-6.
passive	The natural inclination to check or call, a hallmark of many losing poker players. The opposite of **aggressive**.
pocket pair	Two matched **hole cards**; also called a **wired pair**.
position	Where you sit in relation to the **dealer**, which determines how early or late you'll be required to act on each round of betting.

pot committed	The condition of having such a large percentage of your money invested in a particular pot that there's absolutely no point in folding.
pot odds	The amount of money in a pot relative to the size of the bet that you're faced with.
preflop	The time dedicated to action before the community cards are dealt.
premium hands	The most profitable hands in Hold'em, at least before the **flop** (see Chapter Three).
rainbow	A **flop** containing three cards of different suits. This makes it impossible for anyone to draw to a flush on the **turn**.
river	In Texas Hold'em, the fifth and final community card, also known as fifth street.
rock	A **tight-passive** player who may not win very much but who isn't going to lose very much either.

Rules of Four and Two	The percentage chance of completing a particular hand with two cards to come can be approximated by multiplying the number of **outs** by four. With only one card to come, multiply the number of outs by two.
runner-runner flush	A flush completed by two "running" cards—namely the turn and the river. Also called a **backdoor flush**.
satellite	A tournament, often held at a single table, whose winner or winners earn entry to a larger tournament.
scare card	A card whose likelihood of improving or completing a particular hand drives fear into the hearts of those players still in the pot.
semibluff	A bet or raise with a hand that, while probably not the best at the given moment, has **outs**.
set	Three of a kind made with a **pocket pair** and a third card on the **board**. For example, you hold 9-9 and the flop comes Q-9-2.

shorthanded	The condition of playing a less-than-normal number of opponents.
slowplay	To play a strong hand with a deceptive passivity on the early streets in the hopes that your opponents will make (and find the courage to bet) their second-best hands.
small blind	A mandatory fraction of the **small bet** posted before the cards are dealt, usually by the player seated immediately to the left of the dealer.
Smooth-call	To merely call a raise.
stack	The chips that you have in front of you.
stealing the blinds	The act of raising before the **flop** with the intention of persuading the **blinds** to fold.
suckout	The condition (or the verb used to describe the condition: suck out) of betting and losing with what was the best hand . . . until the **river**.
suited	Two **hole cards** of the same suit, the opposite of **offsuit**.

suited connectors	Two consecutive **hole cards** of the same suit. They improve your chances of making straights, flushes, or straight flushes.
supersatellite	A tournament whose winner or winners gain entrance into the **satellite** for a much larger tournament.
table image	The way one is perceived by his or her opponents at the table.
tell	An action or pattern of actions that unintentionally provides information about the strength of your hand to an observant opponent.
tight	The willingness to see **flops** with a narrower than average assortment of hands. The opposite of **loose**.
trips	Three of a kind made with one **hole card** and a pair on the **board**. For example, you hold A-7 and the flop comes 7-7-5.
turn	The fourth community card, also known as fourth street.

under the gun	The player who has to act first before the **flop**.
underbet	The act of betting too little with a made hand, giving opponents the correct **pot odds** to draw for their **outs**.
value bet	A bet, with what you think is the best hand, sized to encourage your opponent(s) to call.
wired	See **pocket pair**.

Phil Gordon is a world-class poker player and teacher who has won two *World Poker Tour* championships, has made five final table appearances at the *World Series of Poker*, and, since 2001, has earned more than $1,700,000 in tournament prize money. His bestselling previous works, *Poker: The Real Deal* and *Phil Gordon's Little Green Book*, along with his teaching and commentary on forty-two episodes of Bravo's *Celebrity Poker Showdown*, make Phil the preeminent poker teacher and writer in the world. Phil currently resides in Las Vegas but spends much time in San Francisco and in third-world travels.